# INVISIBLE TREATS

## POETIC DELICACIES
## FOR THE HUNGRY HEART

TAMEEN FARIDI

Bold Soul Rising

Tameen Faridi
www.TameenFaridi.com

*Invisible Treats*
*Poetic Delicacies for the Hungry Heart*

Cover design: Mumtaz Mustafa

Cover painting by Ayessha Quraishi, 2017
www.ayessha.com

Interior book design: Sara Jamil

Headshot photo of Tameen Faridi: Ayesha Imran

All art used is the sole property of Tameen Faridi

The author of this book does not dispense medical advice or prescribe the use of any techniques as a form of treatment for physical, emotional, or medical problems without the advice of a physician, either directly or indirectly. The intent of the author is only to offer information of a general nature to help you in your quest for emotional and spiritual well-being. In the event you use any of the information in this book for yourself, which is your constitutional right, the author and the publisher assume no responsibility for your actions.

Printed in the United States of America
Kindle Direct Publishing

ISBN-13: 978-0-578-42765-2 (ebook)

SBN-13: 978-0-578-48664-2 (paperback)

Publisher's Cataloging-In-Publication Data
 (Prepared by The Donohue Group, Inc.)

Names: Faridi, Tameen, author.
Title: Invisible treats : poetic delicacies for the hungry heart / Tameen Faridi.
Description: [Paris, France] : Bold Soul Rising, [2019]
Identifiers: ISBN 9780578486642 (paperback) | ISBN 9780578427652 (ebook)
Subjects: LCSH: Mind and body--Miscellanea. | Faridi, Tameen. | Compulsive eating--Miscellanea. | Body image--Miscellanea.
Classification: LCC BF161 .F37 2019 (print) | LCC BF161 (ebook) | DDC 128.2--dc23

*Empowering transformation bridging mind and heart*

# PRAISE FOR INVISIBLE TREATS

"For those wanting to unravel the mysteries of hunger, Tameen Faridi reveals the delicious nourishment to be found in both physical and invisible realms. With her creative blending of prose and poetry with actual recipes, she offers up a feast of insight for the mind, nutritious meals to feed the body, and a heaping serving of inspiration for the soul. If you are seeking freedom from struggles with food and your body, read this book."

**Anita Johnston, PhD**
Author of *Eating in the Light of the Moon*

---

"Tameen Faridi's book is a moving, authentic journey of healing from disordered eating and body dissatisfaction described in prose, poetry, and through recipes. Her poems span the gamut of the emotional, with insights and metaphors on the complexities of our relationship with food, eating, and nourishing ourselves along the transformative journey that healing from an eating disorder entails. She does not neglect the nitty-gritty realities of her own destructive cycle of compulsive emotional eating, binge eating, and body dissatisfaction. But the gentle way in which she probes these wounds allows the reader to follow her along this path from self-loathing to tenderness in a way that is profound and exquisite."

**Carolyn Coker Ross, MD, MPH, CEDS**
Author of *The Emotional Eating Workbook* and The *Food Addiction Workbook*

---

"Tameen Faridi has written a beautiful, haunting book of poetry and prose to explore her journey through and out of her eating disorder. Her words will delight you, stir your emotions, and challenge your mind. I recommend this book for all who are walking a similar path and need a guidebook to support them."

**Elyse Resch, MS, RDN, CEDRD, FAND**
Co-author of *Intuitive Eating* and *The Intuitive Eating Workbook*

---

"There's something unique in Tameen's poems, giving you a safe place to explore the darkest and most pained and longing recesses of our mind in a way that is cathartic, grounded, and beautiful. Food is that most basic requirement for us to live, and it's no surprise therefore that Tameen's poetry is anchored in the imagery and metaphor of this essential part of our humanity. As a descendant of a 12th century Sufi saint, a group who had a unique way of interpreting the universe in words, it's clear that bloodline has remained strong and every bit as insightful."

**Vikas Shah, MBE**
Author of *3650*

"No longer able to ignore her Sufi lineage and the poems singing within her very blood, Tameen Faridi invited them as guests into her heart, fed them with her emotions, and produced this piece of joy. She plumbs the depths of her spirit and our spirit, casting a healing light on her and our own shadows. Writing with a clear and powerful authenticity, the feeling of truth permeates her entire work. She is a new, authentic and direct feminine voice, shining a searchlight on the false pressures of being perfect that the feminine has been imprisoned by. Her book provides a key out of this concrete prison and into the freedom of the fields of Being.

Tameen looks straight into the eye of her Self and writes the unvarnished, un-pretty, un-acceptable truth...and when you are with that, you are freed into a spaciousness of self-acceptance and self-love. Buy this book and nourish your Soul."

**Martin Rutte**
Founder, Project Heaven on Earth

---

"Tameen Faridi has written a gorgeous book, one that will lovingly embrace you with its potent insights, imagery, warmth, and humor. Her poems are delicacies, her recipes soul-satisfying, and the joy in the artwork by her children and mother leaps from the page. Invisible Treats left me humbled, taking me out of my 'scientist' brain to recognize the value of poetry to get inside you and inspire introspection."

**Linda Bacon, PhD**
Author of *Health at Every Size* and *Body Respect*

---

"This lovely collection of poetry, drawings, and recipes offers sustenance and support for those on the path of healing their relationship with food and recovering their love for themselves."

**Judith Blackstone,** founder of the Realization Process
Author of *Trauma and the Unbound Body* and *Belonging Here*

---

"What a wonderful idea! What a wonderful book! Tameen Faridi sings of food but uses it for other-worldly nourishment. This is a striking work, a smoothie of Sufism, self-help, and sustenance. Blending and connection are what this current age is all about, making this book contemporary while remaining true to the author's Sufi heritage. She is following her ancestor Hazrat Baba Farid's advice: 'Do not eat everyone's bread; give everyone bread.' And since we cannot live by bread alone, she adds the treats of prose, drawings, and recipes. Altogether, this book is delicious fun and also greatly thought provoking — a mixture of the enormous and the small. It puts us all in perspective, at the center — but with ourselves lost in the greatness and wonder of the infinite sphere of being."

**Tim Mackintosh-Smith**
Author of *Arabs: A 3,000-Year History of Peoples, Tribes and Empires*

"This is a beautiful book of poetry and inspiration that will delight every reader, not just people struggling with their weight. It's great for every therapist and coach to recommend to their clients, and also, the book is itself therapeutic — plus there are some great recipes."

**Cloe Madanes**
President, Robbins-Madanes Training, author of *Relationship Breakthrough*

---

"Tameen Faridi's book, Invisible Treats, is a lovely feast. Anyone faced with the challenges of eating as a means to assuage emotional issues will love Tameen's heartfelt journey concerning her own struggles with food, body disturbances, and self-esteem. Her compassionate, compelling poems are spiced with homegrown recipes, inviting readers to surrender emotionally and physically to nurturing introspection, understanding, and love. Invisible Treats is a banquet of love, support, and joy. As professionals who have worked with eating disorders for 30+ years and have seen firsthand the damage they cause, it is especially wonderful to find a sister voice of inspiration as we navigate through recovery, consciousness, and acceptance. Invisible Treats offers us a nurturing, delicious, and loving companion on the road to self-love."

**Laurelee Roark, CCHT, and Carol Normandi, LMFT,** Co-founders of Beyond Hunger
Co-authors of *It's Not About Food* and *Over It: A Teens Guide to Ending the Obsession with Food and Weight*

For Buttercup, Nani, and Nana

# TABLE OF DELICACIES

## Menu 2: Magical Spectacles

## Menu 3: It's Not You
A note from the chef – 120

# ACKNOWLEDGMENTS

My poetic journey was made all the easier with the love and
support of family and friends. In particular, I am deeply grateful for the helping hearts of
Tazmeen Faridi Weymuller, Sonia Weymuller, Laila Jamil, Nayyar Jamil, Faiza Kassim,
Seema Alshirawi, Mumtaz Mustafa, Saif Habibullah, Shaheen Liaquat Ali,
Maher Liaquat Ali, Nausheen Farrukh, Malka Ahern, Jyotsna Kaur Habibullah,
Nicole and Joseph Honen, and Nasima Aziz. Deep appreciation to Mehru Jaffer,
who took the time to comment on my book in her wonderful foreword,
as well as to all those who have provided me so graciously with such encouraging
testimonials. I am also thankful to all my dear ones who have stepped
beyond this terrestrial antechamber, but guide and encourage me still.
This includes my dear father, Farid Faridi,
who sadly passed away before publication.

I would also like to thank my editor, David Christel, who upon
being handed a jumble of poems and recipes encouraged me to create a garden path
through this dense, organic undergrowth to make it easier for
the reader to follow my insights. His wise counsel, support and
guidance throughout this process have been invaluable.

Finally, a special thanks to my beloved mother, daughter, and son
whose paintings and sketches sprinkled throughout this offering
provide the perfect ingredients to enrich these poems.

# FOREWORD

Tameen Faridi is a direct descendant of Baba Fariduddin Masud Ganj Shakar, and it is amazing how the spirit of the physical and metaphysical recipes brewed in the kitchen of that 12th century Sufi soul and poet resonate even eight centuries after his death in this marvelous work of Tameen's.

Baba Farid was one of the leaders of the Chishti Sufi Order in South Asia and is loved to this day for his simplicity and wisdom, but above all, for his generosity. The tradition of an open kitchen where food was served to everyone who came to visit Baba Farid begun in his home in Pakpattan, near Lahore, Pakistan, is well known and continues to this day. However, the food Baba Farid had preferred on his plate was contemplation. The wise man had realized early in life that nourishing the spirit matters more, and he never tired of warning himself to always beware of the snare of worldly desires.

Apart from sharing family, what both Baba Farid and Tameen also have in common is a complicated relationship to food. Tameen confesses that for a long time she tried to find acceptance in the world by allowing her diet to disregard her body. Her journey of compulsive, emotional eating lasted for decades until she decided one day to redefine her relationship to food by recognizing the wisdom of nourishing the soul.

Baba Farid's memory has provided Tameen with great food for thought. She spent time wondering what it means to be the descendant of a Sufi saint who hardly ate but lived for over 90 years, making sure that none around him remained hungry. Baba Farid had preferred to fast rather than feast and yet he earned the mouthwatering nickname of Ganjshakar or "storehouse of sugar."

Tameen came across countless stories about her illustrious ancestor that have been cooked up over time into delectable delicacies as to why he is named thus. The tastiest of them is about being so famished after another grueling fast that he tried to ingest pebbles. But those hard talismans turned into roasted sugar in his mouth. In the hands of Baba Farid, stones became the sweet nectar of a deeper knowledge, which he would then generously distribute amongst the many visitors of numerous faiths that always surrounded him.

As Tameen also drank in these stories, the lesson she learnt was to begin by trying to first be compassionate and loving to herself.

She writes:

> How many can begin
> In the here and now
> No matter the shape of their outer skin
> Extending a hand of friendship
> To themselves anyhow

To Baba Farid, the spirit mattered more than the physical appearance of a human being. As Tameen absorbed his wisdom and let rise to the surface the messages already inscribed in her own inheritance, she was able to write poetry that nourished her, lifting the shrouds to profound, universal truths. In her poetry, she has transformed food, that most vital ingredient for life, into a metaphor for individual growth.

After years of compulsive eating, it dawned on her that she was in search of another kind of menu to sustain her heart, mind, and soul as well. She used her imagination to taste the subtle flavors of the invisible world, inspiring her mother, son, and daughter to illustrate her poetic recipes in a book. She concludes that a human being's healthiest diet is wisdom. It is wisdom that leads to basking in the light of the creator of the world.

Baba Farid had preferred the most difficult form of fast in his search for the light of wisdom. He ate only on alternate days. Often, this was a piece of oat bun with ghee while drinking a cup of juice extracted from wild berries. Tameen encourages a more measured, intuitive approach to nourish both the body and soul where the main ingredient remains love.

Tameen is inspired to write:

> The journey is not always easy
> Work is needed, to stay the course
> Because self: love/appreciation/acceptance/trust
> Is the only way through
> To lovely you

Today, the many descendants of Baba Farid are scattered all over South Asia. In Lucknow, there is the family of the late Dr. Abdul Jaleel Faridi, Tameen's paternal grandfather. The Faridi home is still called Shakar Ganj, where the anniversary of Baba Farid's passing is observed to this day. On the fifth day of Muharram, the first month of the Islamic calendar, a sweet kichdi is prepared in a large pot by cooking rice and lentils together and spiced with cardamom, a pinch of saffron, and sugar. The meal is then shared with other members of the community.

That Tameen is well aware of her ancestry is obvious from the healing spirit that infuses every poem in *Invisible Treats: Poetic Delicacies for the Hungry Heart*. It is also mighty generous of the author to have chosen to spread out the fabulous feast of poetic delicacies whipped up by her in this volume so that it can be shared with the whole world.

Bon appetit to all hungry hearts.


**Mehru Jaffer**
Author of *Love and Life in Lucknow: An Imaginary Biography of a City* and several books on the Chishti lineage

# INTRODUCTION

*"Farid, why wanderest thou over wild places*
*Trampling thorns under thy feet?*
*God abides in the heart: seek Him not in lonely wastes."*
Hazrat Baba Farid Masood Ganjshakar

Early in 2017, I sat in a coffee shop on my forty-something birthday, looking back on my wanderings thus far. A reflective introvert by nature, I often had a pen and journal in hand to jot down my musings. Until then, these had taken the shape of long lines of prose, but never condensed bursts of verse. Frankly, I have always been a bit daunted by the prospect of writing poetry. How does one convey the depth of an ocean with just a description of the ripples upon it?

But for some reason that day, a poem slowly emerged. I looked closely and noticed it had a beginning, a middle and an ending, not unlike the short stories I wrote. It allowed me to play with the sounds, textures and rhythms of words, as I created vivid images. Perhaps this was not totally unchartered territory after all. And then I had this crazy thought – to complete a book of poems by my next birthday. I had no idea what it was going to be about nor how I would actualize it. But it had to be done. Once the intention was set, an inexplicable urge to write poetry grew in the following months and I obeyed the call to awaken dormant potentialities.

The whole process of writing has been an organic and cathartic journey. I invited these poems as guests into my heart and fed them with my emotions. We had deep and sometimes painful conversations late into the night. They nourished me, too, with their insights and wisdom, lifting the veils to deeper, universal truths.

One of these is that we enter this world for a special and challenging task, and if we do not perform it, we will have missed out on an exhilarating opportunity. Another is that we were created for self-awareness, and already possess all the necessary tools for it. But work and effort are required to keep alight the creative spark while traveling through darkened crevices. Of course, guides also illuminate the path along the way. In my case, these were books on a wide range of topics, Rumi's poetry, discussions with my daughter who was in her early teens, and numerous intriguing chit chats with my son through his fifth and sixth years.

Themes began to emerge inspired by my everyday life, both past and present, providing rich material to sink my teeth into. An important, and very personal one, centers around the use of food as a coping mechanism to self-soothe and numb uncomfortable and painful emotions. Half my life has been spent thinking about what to eat (or not), trapped in an endless cycle of binge eating and yo-yo dieting. I really did not want to waste what was left of it obsessing any more, while the more I ate, the hungrier I became.

After decades of inner turmoil, it was time to find a path of balance and peace grounded in self-compassion and learning to listen to the subtle whispering of the wants and needs of my physical and emotional bodies. This in turn took me deeper within as clearly food was just a symptom and a veil over a deeper spiritual yearning. Being a direct descendant of a 12th century Sufi saint, Hazrat Baba Farid Masood Ganjshakar, I could no longer ignore the song singing in my blood and began to pay close attention to these mystical notes.

My young son, it seems, was reading from the same musical score. Through what I can only describe as divine grace, he was ready to reveal, and I was ready to listen. I am grateful that I was able to record some of our conversations in these poems. Indeed, perhaps that is one of the reasons why I was compelled to put pen to paper and be a conduit for the healing melodies that arose and waited patiently to be shaped into words and become known.

My daughter, equally, was a vital prompt for my introspections. Her forthright and very perceptive questions and observations encouraged me to explore even more authentically sometimes uncomfortable vistas.

As I tuned into this entrancing harmony, I also took in lessons from all kinds of teachers, including baby lizards, crocodiles, birds, plants, and butterflies. Mundane activities, family dynamics, as well as an embellished tapestry of dreams also fed my original intention to write.

In one such dream, I found myself wondering on a long and busy road. I knew that my journey's end was not far away, yet I kept getting lost. Loved ones who are no longer of this earthly plane appeared along the way and gave me directions, but I remained unable to find my destination even though I was aware that the path was a simple and direct one. I awoke with the phrase "Be still and listen," reverberating in my head. And that is what I did, as these poems became my devotional meditations of remembrance (zikr).

I opened the eyes and ears of my heart and listened in awe. Like loving and gentle anchors, the poems became a reminder that there was another kind of food. And that by relishing this heavenly provision, I could look with humility through magical spectacles and marvel at the miraculous messages at my fingertips, ripe for reciting. It was time to stop the hard eating and start on the voyage of wholehearted living.

Since I do touch upon quite a few areas, with an underlying theme of food as a metaphor for personal growth and awakening, I decided to organize the work into three "Menus." Each is introduced by a preamble or "A note from the chef," to assist in building bridges through the poems to make their digestion easier.

The first Menu, titled "Lovely You," focuses on the key importance of connecting with our inner caretaker, which then provides a safe environment within which to explore the how, when, and what of nourishing sustenance.

The "whys" of compulsive eating are explored in the second Menu, "Magical Spectacles," which goes further underneath the symptom to grapple with deeper territory.

Finally, the third Menu, "It's Not You," goes even further to the root of the yearning for food and centers around spiritual nourishment. Indeed, the "dishes" are all infused with the subtle and gentle flavors of the invisible world.

"Starters" is exactly that, a realization of possibilities with the opening of a door onto new horizons.

"Main Courses" focuses on doing the hard work as the inner alchemy of transformation and integration is accelerated.

"Side Dishes" add richer notes to this process of amalgamation.

"Desserts" gravitates around the sweet and soulful banter I had with my son, although these conversations are also interspersed throughout.

"Drinks" targets family relationships, with those of both this world and the next. These enlightening elixirs are potent vehicles for growth and healing.

I have also included homey recipes for nourishment along the way, to provide some tangible edibles, as well as the intangible sustenance of the poems for the mind, heart, and soul.

I hope you will savor these treats that I offer to you with love, and always remember that what you seek is already within.

# INVISIBLE TREATS

## POETIC DELICACIES
## FOR THE HUNGRY HEART

# INVISIBLE TREATS

Choose
To go forward
And take responsibility
To nurture and care for
Your body
Physically, emotionally, mentally, and spiritually
Close the circle
But be open to receive

No longer stagnant
Choking the entrance
Start moving
On your hands and bloodied knees

Then stand up tall like a stargazer
Enthralled
Follow the Signs
Fortified by invisible treats
Trust in the process
Your path will unfold

First awakening to potentialities
By wearing magical spectacles
Which help you to clarify what path to take
At the crossroads
Or find an exit
Out of the labyrinth
Getting respite at a wellspring
As you follow the seasons

Then accelerating alchemy
Going deeper within
Crawling and sitting
Inside parallel lines
Dotted with houses and cafés

With beautiful mirrors and jasmine trees
Where extinct animals roam freely
Sipping unsweetened tea
Eating fajita rolls and cookies
And despite the indigestion
Relishing the stunning scenery

Continuing on to harmonizing transformations
You remain cognizant of the gap
Between knowing and unknowing
Circles and triangles
And other such magical forms
On this road trip as you fast approach
A sacred space
Beyond the visible
Where reside crocodiles and baby lizards
And unopened gifts
Saying goodbye to old friends
Will not be easy
But there are many more discoveries
To be made

In soulful banter
With profound lessons on angels
And light and bones
Sages and milkshakes
Meditation and recycling
And legends of strange creatures that roam
Deep inside the earth

As you come up for air
Refreshed by enlightening elixirs
Pondering over your sweet genes
Mindfully blaming, grieving, and yearning
For loved ones gone
Upon this infinite road
That you have been called upon
To journey

# MENU ONE

## LOVELY YOU

# A NOTE FROM THE CHEF

My journey of compulsive, emotional eating, binging and see-sawing weight loss and gain have fueled a destructive cycle of body dissatisfaction and low self-esteem for decades. It was easier to shape and control the contours of my body instead of coming face to face with the overwhelm of "doing life." So, I placed the responsibility for my wellbeing by endless dieting into someone else's hands.

Instead of seeing overeating as a signal from a part of myself that needed attention, I felt like an animal trapped in the headlights of painful feelings and ran away from what literally felt like emotional danger into the comforting, welcoming arms of food. Not long afterwards, the yelling from a harsh internal critic left me in tears and feeling worthless, ashamed, and guilty at my lack of will power. All of which were, of course, distractions to underlying issues, as I went back to "fat" and "eating and weight" as all-encompassing, easy labels.

My story is not very different to that of countless others. A child of divorce and remarriage, I was not able to articulate clearly my needs for love and attention. Being very shy and quiet by nature, I became a "goody two shoes" to try and fit in and stuffed down my wishes and desires with food instead. I felt overwhelmed by all the changes that were happening and the core fears of not being enough and therefore unworthy of love took firm hold.

I was already struggling with my weight by the age of 10, and through my difficult teen years and into my twenties, my mother often said that

I "was not comfortable in my skin." The well-intentioned solution was to shrink my skin (i.e., lose the weight) rather than seeking to decode why I was using food.

My dysregulated, compulsive eating fed my isolation and depression and drove me over the edge into trying to end it all. As my life became smaller and smaller, my body became larger and larger, until the burden of the exterior canceled out the nothingness within, squeezing all life out of me.

Decades later, after therapy, an accumulation of life experiences, reading countless books, certifications for life coaching, etc., I felt compelled to assemble some of my thoughts to help others who may need the light of awareness to illuminate their emotional eating, to reach out to those trapped in a dark space where they may have abandoned themselves and let them know that they are not alone. And truthfully, by offering others a path to being in a better relationship with themselves, I continue to heal myself.

It is self-evident that you will only value and look after something you love. Self-contempt never leads to lasting change but rather to further disconnection from ourselves. The cornerstones to reconnecting with our true essence are self-love and compassion, where food is no longer doing the soothing and calming but rather a tender and nurturing internal caretaker is. This means having the patience and courage to unconditionally accept yourself as you are now, not as you will be or should be in some illusionary "perfect" future. The "Treats" in the title of this book therefore also refer to treating yourself with loving kindness.

In *Lovely You,* I encourage you to remember your exquisiteness in non-apologetic boldface. I urge you to see your emotional eating, binging, dieting, purging, using diet pills or laxatives, etc., for the sign posts that they are, at the entrance through which lies your homecoming. So, gather up your perfectionism, shame, and guilt and begin to dive below the still waters of *The Wellspring* of your surface behaviors around eating, relaxing into the flow of life. Then come up for air into an awareness of the present moment to reclaim your voice by singing *An Ode* to the undeniable fact that you are strong enough to be a *Firewalker*.

The path from self-loathing to tenderness is not an easy one. Wanting to become *Extinct* and comfortable in being *Invisible*, it may feel terrifying to genuinely befriend your body, inhabiting it in a non-judgmental way by *Polishing the Mirror* to truly see and honor yourself. And push ahead even if you get *Indigestion*, knowing that you are safe to lift the veil to your deeper cravings and not remain *Unsweetened*.

The next challenge *On Acceptance*, takes you further away from brutalizing thoughts to being present and facing your fears, such as "If I stop dieting, I will become a whale." So that instead of dieting, failing and then rebelling by binging your way out of your eating problems, you savor your way out of them, enjoying *Fajita Rolls*. By decriminalizing "forbidden foods" and focusing instead on tuning into the mindful pause between feeling and eating, satisfy your physical not psychological hunger, with *Hugs and Cookies*. And because you have given yourself a benevolent, comfortable seat at your table laden with nourishing food, you don't mind *Sitting*, watching the ebb and flow of emotions without drowning in them.

With the understanding that real problems cannot be wished away nor camouflaged by dieting, and that a "perfect" exterior shape does not mean a "perfect" life, the illusions behind *The Magical*

*Powers of Form* will be revealed. Until finally, on this odyssey of transformation, you will be able to affectionately let go, with a *Goodbye, Dearest Friend*.

Feeling by feeling, feeding by feeding, this is a slow, gradual process. When faced with resistance and *Tantrums*, enfold yourself in tender acceptance, knowing that these emotional flavors are but transient. Also, don't forget that there is no shame in *Crawling*, it is the parent to bravely walking. Use the minutia of life, like a *School Run*, to flex your muscles of introspection, choosing to catalyze your evolution.

In the final "Desserts" part of this and the two upcoming menus, I continue with this theme of getting inspiration from my everyday life, as these poems center around some of the chit chats I had with my young son. In *An Angel's Appetite*, I explore how inhabiting our bodies is the doorway to coming out of numbness and into feelings by embracing the discomfort rather than eating it away. The importance of being in the present moment and truly enjoying it is the subject of *Meditate and Play*. And finally, a chance meeting with an injured bird in *Undercover Angel* provided fodder for reflecting on wise teachers, metaphors, and freedom.

# STARTERS

# LOVELY YOU

My five-year-old son and I are snuggled together at bedtime
When he looks at me with his bright blue-gray eyes
And eagerly delivers these guidelines:
"Mama, if someone is feeling sad,
they can open your poetry book and read a poem called 'Lovely You.'
And then they will think, 'Oh. I am lovely!'"

Yet, how difficult it is for most
To embody this simple wisdom
So obvious to a little angel
That the prerequisite for change
Is the opposite of self-disdain

How many can begin
In the here and now
No matter the shape of their outer skin
Extending a hand of friendship
To themselves anyhow

How many can see the exquisiteness in their imperfections
Or view their body as a sanctuary
Worthy of tenderness and affection
Rather than the contrary

How many can do life, whatever their size
Because they realize
That when you treasure something
You take wonderful care of it
And this state becomes their default setting
Like breathing

How many can raise their voices
And take responsibility for their choices
Claiming their space with self-assurance
Not in apologetic boldface

How many can see their dysregulated eating
As just a signpost, illuminating:
"Pay attention! Listen to what I have to say.
Tolerate your uncomfortable emotions.
They will show you the way."
That it is not the exit but the entrance

How many can look inside their closets
And contemplate garments of different breadths
Gathering them all up with compassion

How many remember
That hating oneself is far removed
From our original splendor
It is a heavy coat we wear
And can be removed with warm-hearted self-care

How many can hear their own stories with empathy
The shame, perfectionism, guilt, and blame
To see the whole woman of complexity
Not a saintly, unblemished container

This journey is not always easy
Work is needed, to stay the course
Because self: love/appreciation/acceptance/trust
Is the only way through
To lovely you

So, let us begin

# THE WELLSPRING

My daughter tells me she will treasure
These poetry journals once I am dead
And that fills me with great comfort
Because as I slumber
This black ink on white paper
Will continue to be my interface with her

I love the sound of uneven scratching
The flow of rotund cursive writing
With the smooth feel of a longhand implement
And the support of these gray lines
As they witness my many testaments
The messiness of these jottings
Brainstorming, crossing out, putting back in, and other muddlings
Like the ebbs and flows of life's whims

The journey is certainly not linear
It's true, that while I have a final goal to pursue
I am trying not to fall into the trap of perfectionist thinking
Because that is surely a sinkhole
And to creative play, a death knoll

When dieting, I have climbed this all-or-nothing mountain ad nauseam
Reasoning that the faster I lost the kilos
Made me a better person I suppose
That I would shed at least 2.2 pounds per week, with regularity
And that if I did not reach my goal weight by a specific target date
I was a total failure and would be forever horribly overweight

Writing poetry on the other hand
Requires one to take routes often unplanned
By slowing down and pondering
And relishing the scenery instead of running past it panting
Accepting there will be good days and not so good
And in fact, therein are the keys to a deeper learning

It has also opened up new channels of conversation
As my son sits by my side and watches me scribbling
"Mama, can I help you?" he asks
I look up and smile, glad to interrupt my task

"Let's chit-chat and talk about life," he continues
I listen attentively, because I know
That the most profound teachings can indeed come from a five-year-old

"Well Mama, God has told me many things.
But they are very complicated for you.
So, I will tell you just one thing a week," he intones

As I embark on this poetic wellspring
I am eager to see what new vistas the next compositions will bring

# AN ODE TO MY
# FORTY-SOMETHING-YEAR-OLD SELF

Yesterday, you cried
For all the lost years
The heartaches, disappointments and the fears
Feeling sorry for yourself and devoid of sass
As you howled, sitting on your big, fat ass
A prisoner of your victim mentality
Your mind running rampant down dark alleyways
Without your authority

Today, you sing
With the knowledge that your greatest pain IS your greatest gift
Because it is the signpost that will lead to those inner shifts
Towards the magnificence of becoming
It is your Homecoming

So, beat your own drum
And let the world know
That you are ready to glow
Ever brighter
And to help others find their own way out
To shout:

*"I am here. I am ready. I am enough."*

# I AM A FIREWALKER

Immobile, staring at the thunderclouds

Angry, frustrated, and depressed
Meandering aimlessly through the day

Alive, but dead inside

Feeling trapped by your limiting beliefs and
Imagined shortcomings
Refusing to see the stars beyond the gray
Eavesdropping on life rather than living it

Wake up!
Ask the Universe for Alignment
Listen to what She has to say
Keep focused on your passions, not your fears
Energized and taking action
Release the power within

# TASTY TREAT

## MORE MAMA CHEESE SAMOSAS

**For the filling:**

> 250 grams feta cheese
>
> 200 grams halloumi cheese
>
> 150 grams kashkaval cheese
>
> 1 teaspoon dried mint
>
> 1 egg

**For the rest:**

> Samosa wraps
>
> Flour & water paste (the "glue" to seal the samosas)
>
> Oil for frying

1. Grate all the cheeses except the feta. Break the feta into small chunks by hand or knife.
2. Mix all four cheeses with the egg and dried mint. Cheese and mint can be adjusted to taste.
3. Place 1 tablespoon of the cheese mix onto one end of the samosa wrap.
4. Fold into triangles and seal the end with the thick water and flour paste.
5. Fry in a generous quantity of oil (at least 1 inch of oil in a large pan). Make sure the oil is hot first, then reduce the flame to medium high when adding the samosas, ensuring not to overcrowd them. Fry for a few minutes on each side until golden brown and transfer to a plate lined with paper towels to absorb any excess oil.

This makes about 50 samosas and they should be served immediately. We enjoy eating them with some green chutney. To make the green chutney, blend together 100 grams fresh mint leaves, 50 grams green chilies, 150 grams fresh coriander, 1/2-inch piece of ginger, 1 tablespoon cumin seeds, 2 teaspoons salt, and juice of 2 limes.

"HOW MANY
CAN HEAR
THEIR OWN STORIES
WITH EMPATHY?"

# MAIN COURSES

# EXTINCT

In the cavernous, dimly lit chamber
Stand a multitude of species extinct and endangered
Confined within wood and glass, the artistry
Is a masterpiece of taxidermy

"Mama, is that big cat ex-tinct?"
Asks my young son, transfixed
The "Yes" is met by his mournful lament
And his tears soften my heart's callused indents

I begin to wonder about this inner fortification
A place of desolation – a forced incarceration
Restrained and asleep
Is it not time for me to also now weep?

I can no longer live as if deceased!
This is fragmentation, not resting in peace!
It is too heavy a price to pay
For keeping the pain of hurting at bay

But how will I cope with the ramparts being overwhelmed
By memories banished to forgotten realms?
Will I become unglued
To once again turn to my trusty comforter – food?

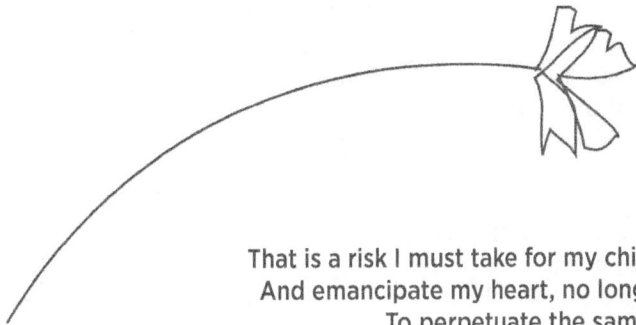

That is a risk I must take for my children's sake
And emancipate my heart, no longer encased
To perpetuate the same omissions
Of previous generations

It is time for traveling into the unknown
This journey can no longer be postponed
From the obscurity whence spirit has flown
Upwards, to the highest Throne
And anchor a new foundation stone

Trusting, that during this reconstruction
Enlightened engineers will provide helpful instructions
To reorient my heart
As it mirrors the Master Builder's art

# INVISIBLE

You choose to be
Unseen, unheard, unknown
Concealed beneath a burnished cloak
Made up of tiny mirrors

A variegated mosaic
In which those around you can see their reflections
So that your own remains unobservable

You might think it is a protective covering
But inside this lonesome abode
Your feelings can get but repressed
Imprisoned underneath that scintillating veil

Until the constriction
Threatens to destroy the mirage
From an implosion of a rainbow of emotions
A treasure no longer buried

To halt this perceived annihilation
This terrifying unmasking
Of your imagined unworthy self
You eat, or not, or both
So that your secrets remain unexposed

The familiar rituals of the insidious habit, the feelings sucker
Numb and distract you from discomforting sentiments
As you spiral back down into insignificance

What a dreary existence!
A slow death as you focus only on the "i" of your own private universe
Unaware and unripe

Since you are already hiding behind a one-way mirror
Why not make use of it?
Tell the Truth to those poor souls
Who see their distorted reflections on the polished veneer

Through their own eyes all they see
Are dreamed up imperfections
Of not being enough
Tell them: "Things are not as they appear."

Why not let the mirrors become a glittering guide
To those travelers overtaken by the night
In a darkened house
So that they may fling open the windows
And turn on the lights

As you look through their facades to the exquisiteness underneath obscured
You will see staring back your own image
Not fragmented, but restored

No longer invisible but
INvisible

# POLISHING THE MIRROR

In the mirror, a misshapen woman
Glares back
Too much flesh squeezed into a
Medium-sized frame
Bulging out
It is the stamp of approval of her shame

She commands me to hide from the world
Her cold stare like fire
Extinguishing any self-control
And I become powerless, not bold

Hypnotizing me onto the path of
Mindless eating
Dotted with signposts:
"Unaware"
"Unseated"
"Unforgiving"

She makes up stories as
We walk down this darkened road together
About how I am not
Thin enough
Focused enough
Smart enough
Pretty enough
And I believe her

Because all I see in the distorted mirror reflected back
Is a woman filled with a deep lack
Of serenity

I want to smash her domination
Into a thousand sparkling fragments
Drifting into annihilation
Right in front of my clouded vision

Instead, I choose to open
The eyes of my heart
And polish the mirror
With a cloth soaked in Love
So that now gazing back at me
Is the face of Infinity

# INDIGESTION

Sometimes, I get terrible indigestion
Of fear and anger, loneliness and depression
Gurgling in my gut, out of control
They keep me awake
Through many a dark night of the soul

I become a gloomy prism
Radiating dimly the muted colors of self-criticism
Trapped in the fragmented house of the powerless
I long to be articulate in the land of the fearless

But instead, I eat
And eat and eat
To distract myself from the discomfort
In my renunciation and inattention, I am triumphant

And so, the pressure builds
As my inner states scream to make contact
To be named and identified
To be recognized

But instead, I eat
And eat and eat
To stuff them back down
Where they cannot make a sound

Until it is not the sentiment itself that causes the heartburn
But my attempts not to feel it that sparks my downturn
Into greater depths of misery
I remain stuck in my story

Could it be that these undigested emotions
Are what will set into motion
My journey towards healing
As I try and decipher their meanings

Are they there for a reason?
Hinting that it is time to change season
From winter into spring
Moving forward into new beginnings

The treatment then is in my own hands
But will I be able to liberate myself from the quicksand?
The comfort of this known territory
Even though rooted in agony
Can exert a strong pull
It is safer to be physically overfull, not hollow
Than come face to face with one's shadows

I take a deep breath and open the door
Because this condition is its own solution
And instead, I feel
And feel and feel

# UNSWEETENED

Food can be a faithful friend
Devoted and comforting
But inducing undigested emotions to belch up:
Not wanted
Not deserving
Not happy

It is much easier to anesthetize
Than go through the pain
But each challenge is a birth pang of awakening
If the ache is not cognizant
Our true self cannot be born
And we remain unfinished

Bellies full or empty
We are undernourished
Feeling secure that by controlling this material form
We become the masters, subjugating all uncertainties

It is nothing but a magic show
Played in our minds
As between sadness and anger we oscillate
Trapped by the gravity of our self-pity
We stay uncoalesced

This food is but a veil
For a deeper craving
A hunger within
A yearning for the Universe
To transmute those parts of us still unhealed
And bring us Home
No longer alone and unconnected

So, do not remain unsweetened
Go seeking Sugar
And open your hearts wide for the precious nectar
Make yourself delicious

# ON ACCEPTANCE

This is one of the hardest lessons
That without acknowledgment
There can be no tenderness
Towards oneself
Both are interdependent
Two sides of the same coin
A yielding with generosity

Does this mean a concession to the status quo?
The answer is a resounding: "No!"
Rather, an allowance of where you are at
Is a prerequisite for a genuine inner makeover
By learning to do life
Whatever your size

This is the paradox
Of welcoming in your greatest fears
"If I stop dieting, I will become a whale."
"If I start eating, I will break the scale."
"How can I embrace myself when I am disgusted with myself?"
Indeed, there may be many more anxious titles on your bookshelf

The fact is that consonance unfolds
Not just through the mind but also the body
And as you start giving your current form Loving recognition
From your brutalizing thoughts taking a vacation
Your tired frame will breathe a sigh of relief
And settle into relaxation
As, miraculously, you find yourself
Approaching an eating equilibrium

So instead of pursuing the "perfect" poundage
Stand quietly and absorb the centimeters
Of your prevailing configuration
Remember, you were not born hating this mold
In fact, you were a lover of the cosmos

Just as a baby cherishes the voice
Of her mama singing off-key
And cuddles into an ample bosom
Like a honeybee
So, no need to wait for society to come around
And appreciate your point of view

Be the star in your own playground
Stay away from judgmental reviews

Acquiescence is not self-delusion
It is instead a pause to listen
And make peace with the present moment
Realizing that by letting go of the desire
To modify your body's measurements
You can put that strength and focus
On your hopes and aspirations
And from a deep slumber, rise and shine

I can already see your face
Recoiling in distaste
At this perhaps uncomfortable hypothesis
But by recognizing and forgiving
Your thoughts, feelings, and contours
Your self
You hold the key
To your freedom from insecurities
And can flow more easily
Into who you are meant to be

Because your eating, or not
Is just a strategy
Developed to cope with living life
Just a history of your past identity
A projection of your mind
Written on the outside
For the whole world to see

But there is an opening
In the neverending loop of oscillating
Between anger/shame and self-pity/blame
Between the yo-yo dieting
And it is called
Acceptance

# FAJITA ROLLS

This is a tale of fajita rolls
Mini Snickers, Twixs, and Mars bars
And how to begin to relish them
Like precious luminescent stars
Without regret nor mayhem

Does this sound too good to be true?
Well, let me tell you
How I have found my way through
So as not to live like a fragmented statue
Around food
And you can decide
Whether or not it will work for you, too

The core issue of this food obsession
Really centers around one key question:
How to deal with the underlying problem
Of overwhelming emotions
Because your chomping through those confections
Is just a symptom

The path does not lie in yet another diet
To distract you from your disquiet
But instead take a deep breath
And plunge right in
To the deep, dark forest
To play the game not with external decrees
But explore what you really need

This means releasing food from
Its sentimental dead weight
So, there is nothing to berate, conflate nor negate
No tags of "good" nor "bad"
To examine instead the whys:
Are you mad, sad, or glad?
Thus, that piece of chocolate cake and those carrot sticks
Become soul mates
With equal breathing space

But sometimes it is easier to feel the sting
Of an empty or overstuffed belly
Than let the ache percolate into your pulsating root
Just the thought may make you unsteady
It is time to stop abusing and start nourishing
Soothing and processing
With tools other than just
Controlling your provisions

The paradox is that it is in eating
That you will make peace with your fasting and feasting
By decriminalizing and legitimizing
All sustenance
Making old enemies available and abundant
So that deprivation can no longer trigger nutrient derangement

Of course, this does not mean an overindulgent free-for-all
Because this requires presence, practice, and patience
Asking your body what it deserves
Not questioning your mind as to what should be required
Feeling into your natural cues of hunger and satiety
This is a journey that spirals
And is not linear
As you trust that each experience will enlighten the interior

There is no need for penance here
Nor playing the martyr
No "Oh, what the hell"
Freeing yourself of dietary restrictions
No testing of boundaries
As between a teenager and caretaker
No battlegrounds to conquer

Moving instead to listening, trusting, honoring
That your body was born already knowing the way
Until the child within was perhaps made fearful and led astray
By well-meaning custodians

The hour has come to make a choice
To heed the call of a deeper voice
As she leads you through the undergrowth
Morsel by morsel

And that is what I have tried to do
When gorging on fajita rolls daily at the school cafeteria
Until my body cried:
"Enough! Not a bite further.
It is time to sit with the discomfort and explore this further.
The rolls will always be there, should I need to sample that juicy fare."

The same held true for the bags
Of mini-chocolates
I had bought more of them than I could digest
And while at first, I sampled too many and felt quite depressed
Bit by bit I savored without judgment

In time, their comforting residence
Made me want them less and less
As I focused more on what I wanted and desired
And whenever my taste buds did salivate
For their sugary marinade
I let myself indulge in one, or two,
Without hullabaloo
Because with my precious time
I had better things to do

And now, when the smiling cashier
At the school cafeteria inquires at pick up time
"No fajita rolls?"
I chuckle and reply
"Not today. Maybe tomorrow!"

# HUGS AND COOKIES

Sitting at a coffee shop having a soy latte
My little son does to me relay
His delight while nibbling on
A triple chocolate cookie
The sweet tidbit for the day

This quiet is a respite from some external frustrations
Not caused by my accompanying playmate, let me add the clarification
And I am still dragging with me negative vibrations
So, I reach for his luscious white and brown biscuit
As my seething resentments
Bubble up from a bottomless pit
I am far from being ensconced
In a self-nurturing space

My craving fingers are stopped short
By a small hand and a quick retort
"Mama, I will give you something much nicer instead!"
And indeed, he does
A long and loving hug

My mindless practice of grasping for food
When in an uncomfortable mood
Is broken by my son's cheeky smile and a kiss
As I hold his comforting body close
And breathe deeply
He then goes back to savoring his treat
Bite by bite
While I ponder on the relevance of the CALM on/off switch

**C**: Compassionate and appreciative thoughts
Towards yourself and body without judgment
As you try to understand and accept your feelings
Putting them into words and examining their meanings
Answering the question: What do you really need?

**A**: Awareness of not only your trigger emotions, but also your body
Is it offering any hints about how you are perceiving?
Is it really hungry, and what does it want feeding?

**L**: Leverage motivators for your breakthroughs
Why are you on this uplifting pathway?
For you? Or your home crew?

**M**: Mindset of making empowered choices
Not automatically driven by habit nor circumstance
But instead a conscious, satiating, and joyous dance
Embracing your life's expanse
In the moment of choice
Between the feeling and the eating
Awaits a mindful pause
Laden with hidden treasure
Of the possibilities of your true measure

# SITTING

Don't let the past weigh down on your shoulders
Nor the future run circles around your mind
Let the present sit quietly in your heart

Become like a little one, with no judgment of right nor wrong
And just observe your life's theme song
Not fighting back, hiding nor numbing
Make a list of all your perceived shortcomings

Listen to the sages
And sit at the bottom of the ladder of ego
Sit outside the mirages you have fashioned of this world
They are but the fancy tricks of your mind
Sit as a woman does the breath before death comes to her assigned
In complete serenity and without distress of all she will leave behind

Sit with the loneliness
And know you are never alone
Sit with the anger
And know it can be fuel for your determination and backbone
Sit with the shame
And know that no one is perfect
Sit with the disappointment
And know that failures are the pathways to becoming a more skilled personal growth architect
Sit with the helplessness
And know it is learned and so can be unlearned
Sit with the confusion
And know it can be a doorway to be transformed
Sit with the fear of not being enough nor worthy of love
And know that Love is already within you, waiting
Sit with the pain
And know that there is only one way out – through it

Sit and listen with your soul
That is the ultimate goal
What do you hear?

# TASTY TREAT  ## CHICKEN AND RICE WITH ADDED SPICE

1000 grams skinless chicken drumsticks (about 12 pieces)

4 large onions, finely chopped

1 cup oil

1½ tablespoons ginger paste

1½ tablespoons garlic paste

2½ teaspoons salt (plus 2 tablespoons when cooking rice)

1½ teaspoons chili powder

2 1-inch cinnamon sticks

3 bay leaves

1 teaspoon cloves

1 teaspoon black peppercorns

3 cups (or approximately 700 grams) of rice

1. Wash the rice and soak it in a large pan of water for about a 1/2 hour.
2. Put oil in a large pan and fry chopped onions on medium heat until light brown.
3. Add ginger and garlic paste and fry for a few minutes until their aroma is released. (I take large quantities of garlic cloves and ginger, grind them separately with a bit of oil in the food processor, and store them in glass jars for general cooking.)
4. Add the salt and chili along with a splash of water, then add the rest of the spices and fry for 3 minutes. The water will prevent the spices from burning.
5. Now add the chicken drumsticks, mix well, and cover to cook on medium heat for 10 minutes. Then open the lid, stirring periodically until the chicken is well browned.
6. In a separate large pan, put 3 cups of pre-washed and pre-soaked rice with 18 cups of water and 2 tablespoons of salt. Cook until tender (taking care not to overcook) and then drain.
7. In a large pan, alternate between layers of the cooked rice and chicken. Close lid tightly and cook on low heat for 7 to 8 minutes.

I like to serve this with some spicy yogurt. Whip 1 cup of yogurt with a teaspoon of roasted and ground cumin seeds, a 1/2 teaspoon salt, 1 teaspoon sugar, a 1/2 teaspoon red chili powder, and 1 teaspoon of *chaat masala* (a ready-made blend of spices available in many grocery stores).

# SIDE DISHES

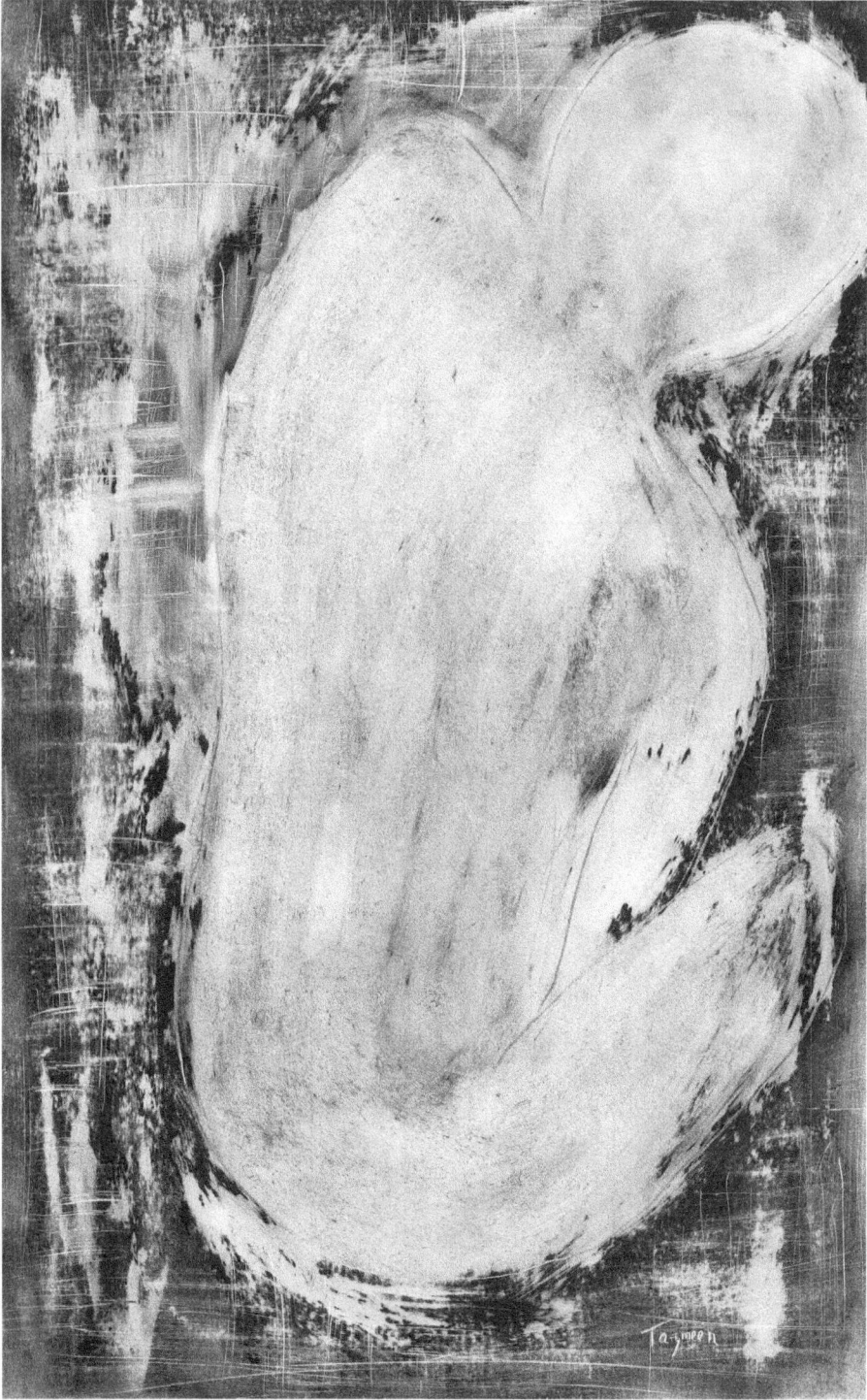

# THE MAGICAL POWERS OF FORM

Come, let's sit awhile
And have a conversation
About any fears you may have
Regarding your transfiguration
And whether it is really fact or fantasy

Being a larger size makes you feel
Powerful and strong like a tree?
The thick branches a manifestation of your suffering
For all the world to see
A safe space to hide yourself
Amongst all the greenery

But paradoxically, also helpless in your invisibility
Letting the world know you are special and need attention
From family, friends, and healers
Because in your own potentiality, you are a disbeliever

You blame your contours
For all of life's detours and failures
And put the future on hold
Until of the number on the scale you are in total control

And yet when the compliments start arriving
You want to send them packing
Not only because you don't feel deserving
But because deep down you want to be accepted as you are
No matter the size, but still a star

"Such a pretty face. If only..."
"If you excel in X, Y, Z, and then only..."

The rage inside you builds against this fine print
And you imagine your dimensions
To be a triumph over all the judgments, critical voices, and oppression
Of "Now, you are a good girl."
And so continues your rebellion

But your worst nightmare might be
That despite reaching your goal weight
People still reject and abandon you
And after all the hard work of your physical breakthroughs
You find that life is still desolate and solitary

You might then assume that there is something defective within
An anomaly in your blueprint
And with no target to incriminate
It is much easier to go back into the arms of a known and familiar enemy
Than venture into unknown territory

There may be other concocted assumptions
We are after all masters at finding excuses for self-destruction
But of utmost importance to remember
Is that this must be a journey into the interior, not exterior

So, don't bequeath your shape a life of its own
In this equation it is you, not it, that has the power
You are the decision maker, the life changer
Not your outline
Its role is but to alert you
To all the hidden meanings that you have given to being fat or thin

It should now be clear that your form has no spellbinding capacity
To grant your wishes of fulfillment nor tranquility
Befriend it, instead of forever in battle
Ask what are its hungers and needs

And as you two sit comfortably and fraternize
The magic will materialize

# Goodbye, Dearest Friend

On this journey of outward transformation
It is useful to question regularly the inner physician
Without whose correct prescription
Even sugar becomes bitter

The Doctor may recommend
That it is advisable to reach out to a compassionate confidante
During this period of mourning
For the loss of a faithful partner

Because that is the role food may so far have been fulfilling
To anesthetize, distract, comfort or punish
Even to nourish
As you went through hard times
It's reliable and unquestioning presence was a life line

Letting go of a close ally is not easy
Especially one that provided so much support, solace and security
To bolt from feelings, block the pain and breathe calmly
Without the fix of that tranquilizer
You will have to learn to trust your inner advisor

The empty space it leaves behind may be filled by a hankering
For all the drama of your seesaw dieting
The thrill of new beginnings
Counting calories, making charts and grocery shopping
Oh, the shimmer of that magical phrase:
"Do you want to lose 10 pounds in 14 days?!"

But as you did the hard work
And the changes became discernible
This "new" you can leave you reeling
So that from this boat you would rather disembark
And eat instead a whole black cherry tart

In the pit of your stomach you may get a feeling
That therein lies a shaded gray ball of yarn, grieving
If you sit quietly a loving voice from within will arise
"Let the silvery threads untangle. Release your fears. I am here."
And like thunderclouds breaking open
You will taste the honeyed nectar
And realize you were always a droplet of the vast Ocean

Or perhaps you could take that yarn and change its color
To rose pink and lavender
To knit yourself a luxurious blanket
And within its abundant folds
Know that even though your teammate may have for now retired
You are neither forgotten nor alone

But a word of warning
This voyage is about progression, not perfection
So don't put yourself up on a food pedestal
Thinking that your onetime friend is no longer accessible
If she does show up at your doorstep
Welcome her in with gratitude and ask
"Why have you come? Let's find out and retrace our footsteps."

Because an unexpected visit from an old companion
Is also a part of the medicine

# TASTY TREAT    MASHED POTATOES WITH NEW FLAVOR NOTES

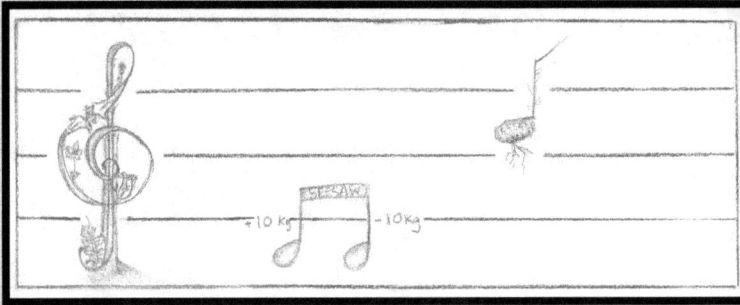

4 medium-sized potatoes

1½ teaspoons salt

1/2 teaspoon red chili powder

1 tablespoon soy sauce

1 teaspoon *chaat masala* (a ready-made blend of spices available in many grocery stores)

1 teaspoon vinegar

4 medium onions, finely chopped

1 teaspoon cumin seeds

2/3 cup oil

1. Boil the potatoes, then mash them.
2. To the mashed potatoes, add the salt, red chili powder, soy sauce, *chaat masala*, and vinegar and mix well.
3. In a medium pan, fry onions until pink.
4. Remove half of the onions and set aside. Fry the other half until golden brown, adding the cumin seeds towards the end to lightly brown also (taking care not to over-brown the latter or else the seeds will taste bitter).
5. To the potato mixture, add the fried onions and cumin seeds, as well as the pink onions set aside earlier and mix all the ingredients well.

This is a zingy alternative to classic mashed potatoes.

# DRINKS

# TANTRUMS

His performance is heavenly
The piercing WAH-WAAAHH!! comes easily
With fat tears, of course, a necessity
And the stomping of little feet thrown in, impeccably

The cloudburst encircles me
Shameless, selfish, single-mindedly self-centered
But at its heart I withstand, like a steadfast tree
Providing umbrage to this treasure, adoringly

He has no interest in finding his positive purpose or setting goals
While moods, behaviors, and attention disappear
Into an unmanageable sinkhole
And forget about brooding over core values, strengths, and needs
Instead he surges between tears to laughter with speed
Confident that mama's affection is guaranteed

How I long for such freedom!
Where there are no more books, courses, nor journaling
Beyond just writing as a way of healing
To feeling, not thinking

In this sacred space
There is no judgment, nor outbursts to be erased
Only tender acceptance
In the knowledge that this is the entrance to grace

Where I can finally allow my cherished little self
To throw a private, petulant fit
No matter the size of it
Conscious that these are but transient flavors
To be savored
With love

# CRAWLING

Sometimes, keen observations
Can come ripping through the fog of introspection
To give a startling description
Of one's metaphorical orientation

Thus, one quiet evening, my pre-teen daughter
Tossed out this electric conversation stopper:
"Mama, you are on your knees. One push and you will be on the floor."
Perhaps it was time not to share with her any more of my poetry
And keep the door tightly shut to all of my vulnerabilities
But I had to investigate

"What do you mean?" I gasped with some trepidation
"You need to get up Mama and stand on your own two feet. Like in your poems."
"Tell me more," I whispered, knowing already where this path was going
"You start out helpless and end up powerful!" she proclaims

It is true, that I may be like a little one learning to crawl
Until I am strong enough to stand up tall
But on this journey, I am owning my story
Pushing the boundaries of my certainties
Trying to practice self-compassion, authenticity, and creativity
Grappling with my fears and imperfections
I am voicing what it means to be human

As I show up in these poems
Letting my tales of worthiness be seen
I will model to my daughter how to honor all the colors of our prisms
So that we can share our struggles and resilience
These are the best lessons I can teach her of life's full-bodied experience

Because there is no shame in crawling
It is the parent to bravely walking

# SCHOOL RUN

This morning I sit appalled
While all around me the traffic is stalled
On the school run

In that moment, my anger is an abstract noun
Denoting a mental state rather than a concrete object
Evidencing my emotional meltdown
But there is nothing hypothetical about it

I feel the indignation fizzing in my bowels
And it twists upwards like a demented scowl
Coating my innards in animosity
It reaches my throat with quick ferocity

The distemper finds form in impatient dialect
As I throw a tantrum, like an aging starlet
Communicating my irritation with gesticulating fists
My displeasure, I just cannot resist

From being a noun, my anger becomes a verb
As my fellow motorists I do disturb
But in both storylines
The vexation is of my own design
Only I can make the effort to find another solution
Since the control is in my hands to catalyze my evolution

Just then comes a wise voice from the back seat
"Mama," proclaims my little one
"If you are angry, the road will be very crowded."
"Oh?" I reply, my interest piqued
"But if you stay calm then the road will be open."

With this intention in my heart
I soften my thoughts, letting the words compose their art
And the following suggestions arise to navigate my path:

1.  Be aware of the annoyance
2.  Acknowledge its prickly presence
3.  Tolerate its nasty jabs into your conscience
4.  Inhale into the discomfort with patience
5.  Be curious, and have with it a loving conversation
6.  Observe it for what it is, a fleeting emotion with no tangible foundation
7.  Thank it for its message, with appreciation
8.  Allow it to dissipate and exhale into relaxation

And just like that, the road opened

# TASTY TREAT

## IT'S A BEAUTY YOGURT SMOOTHIE

500 grams yogurt
1/2 cup sugar
1 glass water
Ice cubes
Mint (optional)

1. Take the yogurt, water, sugar and ice cubes, place them into a blender, and blend for a minute or until well mixed.
2. Add freshly chopped mint to taste.

This cooling yogurt drink is particularly refreshing during the hot summer months. It can also be jazzed up with rose, orange or vanilla etc. essences to give a variety of tantalizing flavors.

"SIT AND LISTEN
TO YOUR SOUL...
WHAT DO YOU HEAR?"

# DESSERTS AND INFUSION

# AN ANGEL'S APPETITE

"Mama, I have an angel's appetite."
Says my little mite
"What?" I am stupefied
The spoon of rice and chicken is put aside

"You called me, so I came down. But I am still half angel and half human."
"Indeed?" I am intrigued
"And you know angels don't eat!"
Comes the response in a heartbeat
"Oh really? But clearly angels like sweets!"
The cherubic face is aglow with a cheeky smile
"Well, that's my human side!"

An ingenious explanation
For picky demands on nutrition
That makes me speculate
About my own emotional relationship to the plate

Enslaved to our body – the human instrument
We drown in diets, detox, and abstinence
Living in fear
That the next kilo up is near

But what if we focused on our angel part
And called upon it through our hearts
To replace the obsessions
With self-compassion
Which needs no material provisions

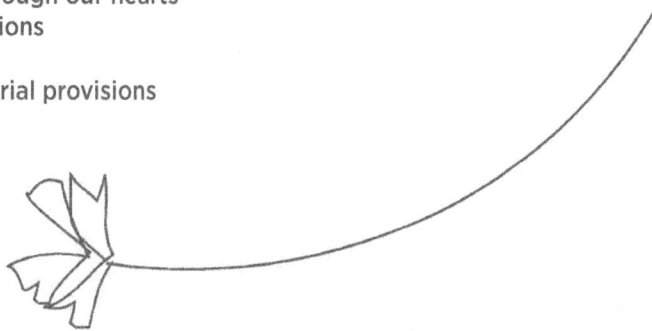

So, instead of punishing the body
We strengthen the soul
To become more Whole
But that is only half the story
As of the corporeal world we are also a repository

Not disembodied, but embodied spirits
Enlightenment does through this physical realm itself exhibit
Inhabiting is the door to feeling
Embracing the discomfort instead of eating
Because we are worthy of occupying this space
As a part of the human race
Sometimes, it takes a child to be reminded of this veracity
Whose stature may be teensy
But whose thoughts are far bigger guests
Than the house of his little body
That we are angel and human both
Manifestly

# MEDITATE AND PLAY

I decide to test out my ankle weights
And give a wakeup call
To the cellulite on my voluptuous thighs
They are my two mates
Whom I affectionately call Harry and Sally
Having given me decades of their loyal company

In this endeavor, my young son wants to partake
Helping me smooth out a pale bed sheet
On the comfy turquoise and yellow rug
I suggest we start out with some stretching
And when I begin to show him how
He furrows his pensive brow
And comes up with an agenda of his own making
Which goes something like this:
Meditating; running around in circles ten times;
letting me use the ankle weights;
boxing the settee (like Muhammed Ali)
And finally, playing a game of hide and seek

I laugh and ask who taught him to meditate
With a "Oh, Mama!" look in his eyes
He sighs and patiently replies
"Your soul teaches you how to do it, of course!"
I am mesmerized

But although his soul may be old
His body is still five years all told
And after sitting still hardly a minute
He is soon fidgeting with movement
So, we continue on our course

Sometimes there is no point in reasoning
Indeed, as wise teachers warn us
That can be like poison to Awakening
Rationalizing is fine until it brings
An ailing patient to the Physician
Thereafter, she must surrender
To the Healer's expert skills

And as I was reminded by my son
All the instructions necessary
Are already within
So, breathe deeply
Don't take life too seriously
It's time to play

# UNDERCOVER ANGEL

"Mama, that's not an undercover angel. It's just a bird!"
"Excuse me?"
I looked at my son, confused by this unasked-for confirmation
"You know, an angel in disguise! Here to take you back up. Or to warn you. Or tell you what's going to
happen in the future," he continued impatiently
Through my reverie were these curious words heard
As we contemplated the injured feathered creature
Trembling behind the flower pots, stunned and in pain

It had barreled into our closed bay windows with a loud thud at full speed
And badly misjudged the solid obstacle indeed
Hurtling back down from 20 meters to hard ground
Where, writhing in pain, it was then found

With graceful white plumage
And what looked like a dark, cinnamon-colored waistcoat
And coffee-bean eyes that seemed to affirm:
"Pay heed, this meeting is an important anecdote."

When my sight first fell upon it, I was filled with dread
Immobile at my doorstep, I thought the beautiful dove was dead
Which did not bode well for my homestead
I hoped I had the signs misread
And sure enough, it pushed itself up
Winking at me, relieved

Gently, I took my wounded companion
And placed it in a pet carrier, to rest and recuperate
With water and sustenance
Until it would to me intimate
That it was healed and ready to ascend

Wise scholars have embraced the bird as an emblem
To denote the human soul on its spiritual journey Home
The constriction and extension of bird wings
Like the shrinkings and elations this odyssey of life brings
But the choice whether to stay caged
Or fly to Freedom and listen to our soul's song
Remains ours, as we travel alone

So, I wondered what message this guide, even if not an angel, had for me
Because the light of knowledge
Is to be gathered grain by grain
From every teacher and every friend
Who are like rays of the Original Sun
Calling from a far-off abode

Perhaps it was time for me also to reflect and re-energize
Before taking flight

# TASTY TREAT     ## NO COUNTING CALORIES BROWNIES

200 grams of 70% dark chocolate

200 grams butter

2 cups sugar

4 eggs

2 teaspoons vanilla essence

1/4 cup flour

1/2 teaspoon salt

9 x 13-inch pan for baking

1.  Pre-heat oven to 180 degrees Celsius. Grease a 9 x 13-inch pan.

2.  In a medium-size saucepan, melt and stir the chocolate, butter, and sugar together on low heat. Then pour into bowl and allow to cool for a bit.

3.  Add the eggs, vanilla essence, flour, and salt to the melted chocolate mixture and whisk together. Spread into prepared pan.

4.  Bake in pre-heated oven for 25 to 30 minutes, taking care not to over-bake.

My children love this simple brownie recipe and it is also a favorite amongst their friends!

# INFUSION

## LEMONGRASS ICED TEA

3 stalks of lemongrass with trimmed stalks and tops (plus extra for garnish)

1 large lemon (plus extra for garnish)

3 tablespoons brown sugar

1 tablespoon loose leaf tea (for example, Darjeeling)

1-liter jug of cold water

Ice cubes

Organic honey to taste

1. Bruise lemongrass stalks gently and boil them with 3/4 cup of water for 5 minutes on medium heat, then take the pan off the fire and remove the stalks. Add in the sugar and stir to dissolve.

2. Add the tea leaves, stir, and allow to infuse covered for 5 minutes and then strain. Combine the tea and lemongrass mixture with the jug of water, then add the lemon juice and lemon rind and stir well.

This drink is so refreshing after a spice-heavy meal. Serve with a few cubes of ice in tall glasses and add organic honey to taste, as well as a garnish of lemongrass stalks and slices of lemon.

"...FLY TO
FREEDOM
AND LISTEN
TO OUR
SOUL'S SONG"

# MENU TWO

## MAGICAL SPECTACLES

# A NOTE FROM THE CHEF

You are now on the path to giving yourself permission to take care of your hunger and your body in compassionate ways, with the consequent decrease in emotional hunger. There is more attuned nurturing, delinking your eating from your body size, along with frequent experiences focusing on internal cues of hunger and fullness. Your confidence in non-judgmental, self-caretaking is also slowly taking hold. You can thus pause during destructive eating patterns and choose to take responsibility, finding satisfaction and pleasure in food, while moving away from deprivation.

Nonetheless, you may still find yourself in front of the fridge at 3 a.m. gorging on ice cream, sometimes not even knowing why, or perhaps unable to comfort yourself in other ways. Because the walk and bubble bath taken earlier that evening were just not enough of a distraction from a lingering emotional storm. Thus, you continue to be caught in the paradox of wanting to heal and grow, yet not done craving some certainty, as well as wanting to avoid pain.

However, pain, unhappiness, loss, and discomfort are a part of the human experience. Indeed, these are the pungent spices that will compel you to gulp down the cooling nectar of awareness, which in turn offers a remedy to true healing. But suffering is caused by your inability to accept this truth, and instead you allow it to trigger negative and self-critical thoughts that color your interpretation (or story) of the situation. This in turn causes your mind to be flooded with feelings of helplessness and hopelessness.

Meanwhile, you are trapped in your behaviors (dysregulated eating), becoming disconnected from the best emotion revealer on the planet — your body. Now, it is time for a deeper awareness and allowing, to start investigating, with kindness and curiosity, what is really going on underneath the suffering, and finally break free from the prison of your negative core beliefs.

These beliefs about oneself are often formed at an early age and play a critical role in the creation and maintenance of eating disorders. In my case, they coalesced during times of emotional upheaval and transition during my childhood and adolescence. I felt overwhelming emotions during my parents' divorce and in the subsequent reorganization of their lives, using food to numb and soothe as a coping mechanism. My sense of isolation and unworthiness was compounded by my shy and introverted nature, as well-intentioned adults often told me that I "stared too much at my navel," focusing more on my achievements and how I was *doing* rather than how I was *being*. I also sought love and acceptance by remaining a "good girl." And of course, good girls don't get angry, make demands, nor raise their voice.

In these poems, I have found my voice, to explore forbidden feelings with kindness, welcoming in and conversing with those aspects of myself I had previously gorged down. Moving away from the twin pillars of guilt and shame that have kept aloft my compulsive eating, I chose to move towards honest inquiry around their survival with curiosity instead.

*Magical Spectacles* extends the invitation to begin this decoding, to decipher the deeper landscapes beneath. The importance of *Breathing* through the heart rather than being stuck in the fear-based mind is a crucial skill on this journey. As is of course continuing to be ensconced in compassion and patience through the *Seasons*, as your path unfolds. It can be an exhilarating process, as demonstrated in *Antechambers 1, 2 and 3*, where we lovingly gather together all our facets springing forth from internalized family and cultural beliefs and let them be honored and heard with the help of the inner caretaker.

Then, peeling away even more layers, we uncover a kaleidoscope of self-discoveries in *The Neverending House*. The suffering caused by turning away from our pain is explored in *The Split Self Café*, as our fragmented selves embrace the present moment instead and step into wholeness. This theme is examined also in *Baby Lizards*, underlining the importance of allowing rather than discarding what you may perceive as "the monster within."

Instead of feeling like there is something wrong with you and believing that you are powerless and worthless when vulnerable or unsafe, take the hand of the little one and go on a *Road Trip* together. Relish the beauty and truth contained within *The Unopened Gift*, knowing that through the joyous creativity of magical thinking you will find the solution. Inside a dream, where *Circles and Triangles* are two halves within a perfect whole, not mismatched pieces in a circumference.

These universal shapes also appear in family constellations, starting with two and then becoming three. This is the theme of the poems in the "Drinks" section of this Menu. *Sweet Genes* delves into my Sufi ancestry, while *Four*, *25 Years*, and *Mindfully Playing the Blame Game* elaborate on this family focus further — in particular, exploring the recent reconnection with my dear father after many years of estrangement.

Owning and facing painful life events with compassion takes courage, and is necessary for letting go of the past, making the *Sunrise* all the sweeter. Finally, there is also a deeper appreciation for the *Legacy* that will be left behind.

The final section of this Menu is again infused with some enlightening exchanges I had with my son. Thus, I encourage you to be open and be present to all experiences as *Opportunities* for growth, because life is both sweet and salty. Remaining in flow by doing what you love is also important, even if that means *Chasing Crocodiles*. Finally, I heard *The Legend of the Millipede Runner* from my young son's perspective, and upon further reflection found this tale to be a multi-layered treasure trove of metaphors.

Writing the latter, and many other poems that appear in this compilation, was truly an exercise in tuning into the gentle whisperings of the Beloved. This trust and heart-opening would not have been possible had my mind still been in the emotional fog of my compulsive behaviors. I suppose the Beloved knew this time would eventually arrive, even if I did not, when I would be ready to listen to my young son's otherworldly musings, even though I may not yet completely comprehend them. For example, he told me with great seriousness one day, "Mama, all living things are linked and they are inside a large circle. Then inside this large circle there are smaller circles touching each other, for different species, like plants and animals. And these touching circles cannot be broken, except by God or the angels."

In Menu 3, we delve further into this final piece of the puzzle — the yearning underneath our quest for nourishment, for connection to something much larger than our small selves.

# STARTERS

# MAGICAL SPECTACLES

Lying down in the garden enjoying the breeze
I look up at the twinkling sky
To witness an incredible sight
Fluffy, white clouds in the shape of my spectacles
Are floating gently by
Past the orb of the luminescent moon
I breathe in deeply
And feel their healing presence most keenly
As a hint
Placed before my eyes by exquisite design

Cocooned in the darkness of the night
I marvel at this singular display
Wondering what their presence is here to demonstrate
What new landscapes would appear
Through that magical line of sight?

Could they:
Uncover abandoned and neglected parts of myself?
Be used to peer into the hidden darkness to reveal the light?
Decipher the ancient language of images and archetypes?
Be a doorway to subtleties within which resides the Wise Woman?
Let me put aside my own glasses with the distorted lens
And look instead through more compassionate ones?
Disclose my unique path to the sacred space within,
harmonized to my soul's beat?
Expose the daily signs of all my Invisible treats?

In the stillness
An elation arises within, unbidden
God is playing a prank
To my shroud of slumber giving a gentle yank

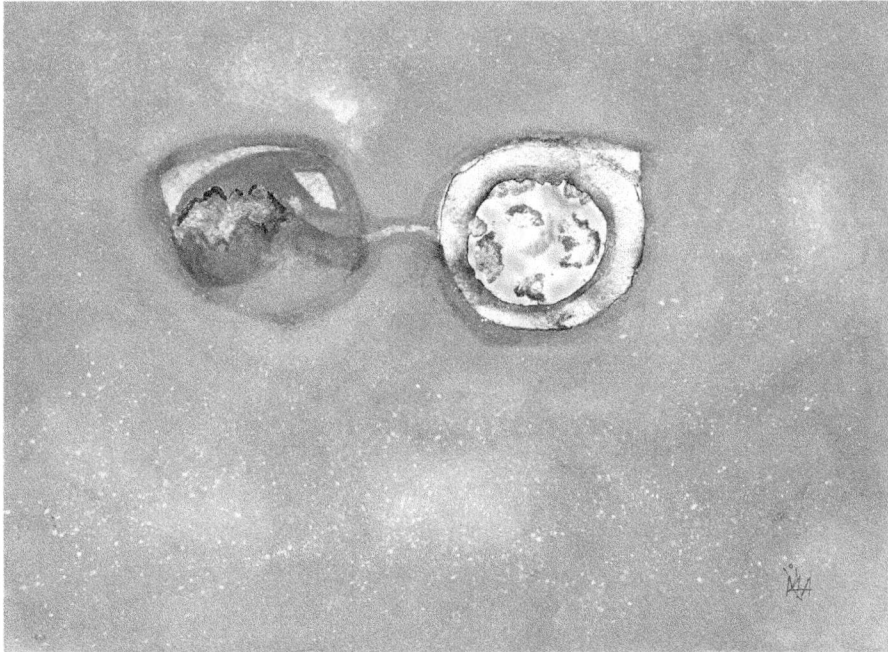

Declaring:
"Open the eyes of your heart!
Polish the mirror so that you may see more clearly
All the synchronicities and gifts I give to you freely.
They are not meant to stunt but to make you grow!"

But as I observe the magical spectacles
Soaring off into the distance
I am struck with the paradox
That although I may think I have perceptive vision
Really, I know nothing
And that this is a lifelong adventure
Of a hungry beginner

# BREATHING

Knowledge may be inhaled and exhaled through your mind
But knowing may only be breathed
Through the
Heart

The mind is where fear dwells
Even though it may sometimes feel
Like the terror is in your heart
Because of the palpitations
You cannot quell

Go into your fear
At its center is the Light
Let it be your guide
Remembering to
Breathe
All the while

# SEASONS

Starters
Main courses
Desserts
Side dishes and Drinks

Physical
Emotional
Intellectual
Spiritual

Surfacing
Breathing
Plunging
Deepening

Fear
Shame
Blame
Surrender

A call
The quest
Trials and ordeals
Rebirth

Lose 3 kilos
Put on 4 kilos
Lose 5 kilos
Put on 7 kilos

Feelings
Moment of choice
Mindful pause
Intuitive eating

Spring
Summer
Autumn
Winter

# TASTY TREAT

## GET-OUT-OF-BED SPICY EGGS

1 tablespoon garlic paste

1/4 teaspoon turmeric powder

1 teaspoon salt (or more to taste)

1 teaspoon red chili powder (or more to taste)

1 teaspoon fenugreek seeds

360 grams whipped yogurt

6 eggs

1 cup water

1/4 cup oil

1. Mix the garlic paste, turmeric powder, salt, and red chili powder with the water until thoroughly combined.
2. In oil, fry the fenugreek seeds on medium heat until light brown. Ensure not to over fry as they will then become bitter.
3. Add the spice mixture to fried seeds and keep stirring for a few minutes until the oil rises to the surface.
4. Add whipped yogurt.
5. Pour in eggs without whisking and cover. Do not stir. Leave to cook on a low flame for 15 minutes. Take the cover off and cook until most of the water has evaporated, ensuring the egg yolks have cooked through.

This is a great alternative to omelets for a weekend brunch. It is also delicious as a filling for school sandwiches, mixed with some light cheese, or on crackers as a snack.

# "OPEN THE EYES OF YOUR HEART!"

# MAIN COURSES

# THE ANTECHAMBER, PART 1

I am sitting in a brightly lit room
With four empty chairs, waiting to be filled, I presume
On the wall is a striking portrait
Of an intermingling: air, water, fire, and earth
What a strange amalgamation
Of simplicity and contemplation
And below it a caption: "All will be revealed."

I am lost in thought when comes the sound of a measured knock
And in marches from the antechamber – me
Dressed in dark gray pantsuit
With a pearl necklace and sensible shoes
"Greetings. My name is Goody."
"Indeed?" I reply, intrigued

She has barely taken her seat
When there is an animated banging on the door
"Am I on the correct floor?" bellows a high-pitched voice
"Oh, my word," I am stunned
There stands a second replica of us
In comfy flip flops and a sparkling pink scarf
And a white t-shirt with gold lettering: "You are the One"
She saunters in and gives us each a fervent hug
"It's so amazing to meet you both. My name is Fizza.
This is going to be such fun!"

As the new arrival jumps into a chair, there is yet another knock
So soft, we can barely hear it at first

And in glides me, part three
In a billowy aquamarine-colored dress
With a sizable chocolate fudge cake
With which we are all impressed
"Hello my dears. I am Amoretta," she smiles warmly
Giving us each a tender kiss on the cheek

So, we convene, a circle of sisters
Humming with questions and some jitters
Wondering – what's next?

# THE ANTECHAMBER, PART 2

We remain together in silence
Goody, Fizza, Amoretta and I
All ogling the chocolate fudge cake
Our stomachs are rumbling with a dull ache
This yearning at least we share in common
And smiling at each other, our faces blossom

Fizza bounds forward and picks up the knife
Her rotund body at ease
She looks like the kind of woman who does as she pleases
"Oh, for heaven's sake!" her brightly colored bangles jingle to life
"Now who wants a big, fat slice? Let's enjoy this scrumptious gift!"

Sinking further into her seat
Goody eyes Fizza with a horrified glare
All she can see are her bulky thighs spilling over the sides of the chair
But not wanting to hurt anyone's feelings
In a quiet voice she pleads for just a tiny portion
Scolding herself as one would a small child
That there would be no second morsel

Amoretta beams, sitting comfortably in her shapeless attire
And turns to me, inquisitively
My ambivalence soon evaporates, doused by her firm stare
"It's my new recipe, do try it dear," she croons
But in my head, I hear: "I slogged over this. Just shut up and eat it you fool!"

She ambles towards Fizza who has appointed herself as the unofficial hostess
"Give me a generous slice, whatever you do.
With a nice cup of hot tea.
And Goody, come here and sit by me. Let's get cozy."

And so, I watch the three of them
Fizza and Amoretta on each side with Goody in between
Relaxed and giggling with their pleasantries
With Amoretta patting Goody on the head lovingly
While Fizza adorns Goody's empty wrists with some of her own accessories
I feel satiated and start drifting off into a contented reverie

The tranquil air is soon shattered by more strong, persistent knocking
And in strides a fourth me in army fatigues
Hair pulled back in a tight bun and shoulders linear
She shakes each hand in a firm grip, and I wonder if she is skinnier
"Good morning ladies! Name is Ripley."

# THE ANTECHAMBER, PART 3

So, there we are
Goody, Amoretta, Fizza, Ripley, and I
Staring at each other, tongue-tied

Fizza is the first to make a move
Her hips swaying in a beguiling groove
With an engaging smile, curious and accepting
She gives Ripley a warm-hearted embrace
And of distrust there is not a trace

For a moment, Ripley's square shoulders become a soft curve
Her fettered chest relaxing without reserve
As she lets her guard down
While Fizza, with a gentle hand caresses her defensive frown

Amoretta is having none of it
And with a protective shove
Shields Goody behind her heaving exterior
Ripley's patriarchal countenance whips up her emotions into a blur
Of indignation and derision
She eyes the new arrival with suspicion, barely contained

Goody peeks out from behind Amoretta's shoulder

And after giving Ripley a soft-hearted smile
Guides Amoretta to a small table in the corner
That seems to have been there all the while

On it is a medium-sized, smooth black stone
Goody heaves it up and gives it to Amoretta
Who clutches the rounded edges with a soft moan
And as her tired back crumbles
The tearful release from deep within her frozen heart is full blown

"No need to carry it any longer, my love," whispers Goody
Her supportive arms around Amoretta are motherly
And gently prying away the mineral
She magically replaces it with a golden receptacle

It is filled with the radiance of multi-colored rose petals
And with their perfumed scent
A calm and restored air on Amoretta does descend
As she explores their cooling texture in her hands
Awareness to the present moment do their healing properties command

Fizza's squeal of delight pauses
Everyone's keen attention on Amoretta's breakthroughs
And as one, we turn to discover
A cheerful fireplace aglow
With five comfortable chairs all in a row

Goody and Amoretta take up residence
In the first two seats on the right, without hesitance
Followed next by an animated Fizza
Who has to drag a reticent Ripley with her
That leaves just me, but as I move
Towards these waiting characters
I notice an object on the table
There awaits a pretty gift box with glittery lettering:

*For dearest Amoretta,*

*Knitting tools to create a cozy blanket. With unlimited yarn!*
*Much love and light,*
*Xoxoxo*

I give the precious offering to its intended beneficiary
And in return am handed the golden repository
The aroma of rose petals is intoxicating
As I take my assigned seat
I can feel my heart peacefully pulsating

Ripley, who is fidgeting next to me
Seems far from content
So, I pass her the vessel
Hoping this restlessness
The mystical touch of the petals will circumvent

But Fizza has a much better perception
Noticing that Ripley still has on
Her big, clunky boots, the ungainly contraptions
She coaxes her to be free of them
As well as the thick gray socks
And Ripley wiggles by the warm fire her calloused toes
No longer feeling boxed
But able to breathe in instead
The rejuvenating fragrance of the roses
Meanwhile, Amoretta has been knitting up a storm
With the salmon-colored yarn
And starting from Goody nuzzled next to her
She begins with the snug blanket to adorn
Then it is compassionately passed on
To each manifestation of myself
And we all have the soft mantle in abundance

So, dear reader, take time to also sit with your cherished selves
At the desk, on the bus, train, or airplane
While you drive your children to and from school, changing lanes
In a mountain lodge, immersed in creation
Or in a beach hut, breezy and sparkling
But most of all when feeling totally alone
Take deep breaths and quiet your mind
Limited in space and yet unconfined
Become a circle of sisters
Ensconced in Grace

# THE NEVERENDING HOUSE

There is a stately manor
Of many-colored hues
Containing countless rooms with stunning views
Of a blissful garden like no other

Inside each sheltered space
Extraordinary amalgamations are taking place
Of the five senses an alchemizing
Sight, sound, taste, touch, and hearing
To get complete and welcome a new, sixth reality

Like five personalities coming together
Goody, Amoretta, Ripley, myself, and Fizza
Individual petals from the same tea-pink rose
Co-existent to become but one shadow

A cast of characters
The Maiden, Matriarch, Amazon, Mystic, and Seductress
Sitting in a cozy room
As snug as a growing baby in the womb
Warming our feet by roaring flames with iridescent red-yellow plumes

Five facets of one soul
Emotions, mind, ego, heart, and body
All coalescing for the same goal
To remember our true Identity

This quest of rediscovery
Reclaiming all our scattered fragments
Requires much courage and patience

Not to fall into the trap of
Anxiety
Passivity
Rigidity
Sentimentality
Pomposity
Anesthetized by this playing small
Unable to imagine what lies waiting on the other side of these four walls

Not realizing that we are so much more
A kaleidoscope of selves
Strengthening
Nourishing
Supporting
Contributing
Understanding
Each other

Students engaged in the dance of balancing all these gifts
To actualize the inner shifts
That will unlock the door
To our deepest core

Because in this classroom
There is an opening
Beyond which lies a rose garden wherein birds soar
Bathed in the light of an eternal lamp
Fueled by the fire of remembrance

But this doorway to the ultimate reality
Can only be opened by divine decree
With the very special key
Of Mercy

This antechamber is but a vestibule
For growth and becoming, it is a school
If we so choose
In order to be blessed with an invitation
And become guests
At the Neverending House
Within

# THE SPLIT SELF CAFÉ

I received a most curious artifact this morning
A vintage, beige-colored envelope
With a wax seal emblazoned with "T&T"
A dinosaur in this age of technology
That was not quite so easy to swiftly delete
And the contents of which I, with trepidation,
Did proceed to read

> *My Dearest Twin,*
> *Please do join me tonight at 7pm for an evening of nourishment and conversation at the Split Self Café.*
> *It is time.*
> *With love,*
> *Your Shadow Sister*

At the appointed hour, I made my way
To the mesmeric eatery by the sea
Through fairy lights that formed a sparkling gateway
I arrived at an intimate space
Of pink rose and lavender
And there she reclined, waiting patiently
My carbon copy

Any hesitations she dissolved in her affectionate squeeze
As we sat down to a scrumptious feast
And she began to recount her tale
Or rather, our journey through life's arduous vale

She described herself as the keeper
The guardian of the inner world
Of all our insecurities and fears

Those "bad qualities" labeled as such by others
We had repressed for years and years
Of being too loud; too selfish; too intuitive; too outspoken; too questioning; too powerful;
too needy; too weak
But the fact that I was by her side
Meant that I was now ready to take this liberating ride

Through my "fog of illusion"
She opened a doorway of consciousness
And painstakingly went over the evidence
Of how I agonized over counting calories
Rather than feeling the pain of seeing myself
As wrong, damaged, and unworthy

How I began to split off from wholeness
My birthright
To become trapped in the shoulds
As I ran headlong into the dark night
Of self-doubt and loathing
After each inevitable failure at yo-yo dieting
Shamed by the monster of helplessness and lack of willpower
The light of my authentic self grew dimmer by the hour

And so, the more I denied and rejected
The greater a sense of injustice, arrogance, blame and defensiveness I projected
As a barricade to self-examination
The deeper grew my food obsession
I forgot who I was
Stuck in the stories I made up about myself
I slowly became my own greatest victim

I then held my shadow sister's hand and became overwhelmed
With the ache of unfulfilled dreams and lost opportunities
The sting of self-judgment transmuted to sympathy
And as self-compassion reached deep into my heart
My dark twin leaned forward and gently began removing my many masks

With vulnerability and empathy
We continued to talk through the night
Under the blessing of the full moon, ever so bright
I thanked my sister for her gifts
Of teaching me acceptance and forgiveness
And disclosing all the nooks and crannies where I was still incomplete

With the first rays of dawn
We pledged our everlasting friendship
Determined to work through this process
Of kind-heartedly putting back together all the pieces
Making up the unique mosaic
Of our emotional body
No longer separate but One
As we were always meant to be

# BABY LIZARDS

We stare at each other cautiously
As I sit writing poetry
64 inches of me and 2 inches of her
This is my second encounter this past week
With an animal that has frankly always given me the creeps

The slithering beige form with its webbed feet
Has since my childhood seemed to me a disgusting beast
Making my skin crawl and toes convolute
With an inexplicable desire to puke

But this time, as I did with its predecessor
In haste, I grasp a dustpan and brush
Then gently nudge the baby lizard from the floor into this ambush
And with the bile rising in my throat
I head out of the house and into the garden
To liberate the petrified mote

As I observe her crawling into the welcoming grass
I proceed to myself this question ask:
What lesson am I supposed to learn from this small reptile that triggers my revulsion?
Because each encounter in life can be a gift for self-exploration

"Baby" and "Lizard" seem to me like two words quite juxtaposed
Insinuating different things to suppose
Baby: cherubic, innocent, pure, celestial
Lizard: monstrous, grotesque, impure, fiendish
The cherished divine child versus our disowned shadow

Yet, it is our childhood terrors
That often give birth to our darkened shield
When from painful moments we are not healed
And begin to believe the myth
That we have a gargoyle lurking within

Not being "enough" of anything
Some turn to food to fill these hollow expanses
Constructing towering walls to protect fragile heart spaces
Until we forget our true faces

That we were once babies who turned away from our mothers' breasts
When our bodies knew they had received enough sustenance
That our emotions were fully experienced and expressed
And nothing was repressed
But as the shadow sister grew stronger
There was more self-hate and judgments
With erroneous beliefs that self-reproach would miraculously lead to self-improvement
No longer trusting natural appetites, but rather what the next diet commanded instead

It is often those things we think of as destructors
Which become our best instructors
And the more we reject and suppress the ogre
The more we will find it becoming a recurrent fixture

The Universe is psychedelic
And so do we have many shades
It is time to let both the little angel and monstrosity play
In the Garden of the Soul without delay

# TASTY TREAT

## "I AM THE BOSS" SPAGHETTI WITH A DELICIOUS SAUCE

500 grams minced beef

1 large onion, finely chopped

1½ teaspoons garlic paste

2 teaspoons pesto

1 teaspoon dried rosemary

1 teaspoon Italian herbs

1 beef stock cube

Salt and pepper to taste

3 tins peeled tomatoes

3 tablespoons tomato paste

10 fresh basil leaves

2 cups hot milk

1/4 cup olive oil

Spaghetti

2 tablespoons butter

Parmesan Cheese

1. Heat oil in a medium pan. Add finely chopped onion and fry on medium-high heat until light golden.

2. Add garlic paste and fry until aroma released. Now add the minced meat and continue to fry until browned.

3. Add pesto, dried rosemary, Italian herbs, crumbled beef stock cube, salt and pepper to taste, and fry further for about 10 minutes with 1/2 a cup of water.

4. Now add the peeled plum tomatoes and tomato paste and cook for 5 to 10 minutes.

5. Add basil leaves and hot milk. Mix well and bring to a boil. Then leave to simmer, covered on very low heat for about 30 minutes, or until the oil rises to the surface. Taste, and adjust the seasoning as needed.

6. Separately cook the spaghetti in a large pan of water, with a pinch of salt and 1 tablespoon of olive oil. Cook according to the packet instructions. Once done, drain and add back to the pan with a knob of butter and stir.

Plate up the sauce and spaghetti, sprinkling with shaved parmesan cheese. I freeze the sauce in individual-sized portions to use as and when needed — which is quite often as my children love this dish!

# SIDE DISHES

# ROAD TRIP

Last night, I had a dream
That I was sitting in the back seat
Of my Honda CRV
Being driven by little me

Jet black hair bobbing in ringlets
A sweet smile illuminating the rotund face
There she sat in a soft, pink dress
With a necklace of tiny, white pearls
Ready for this journey to unfurl

My mind at first choked
Was this a joke?
How could a child take this responsibility?
Did she even know all the rules and regulations
That were needed to get us to our destination?

Sensing my trepidation
She chirped up with exhilaration
"Don't worry, I have got this!"
And as the car moved smoothly forward
She opened the glove box
To retrieve a huge slice of chocolate fudge cake

I stared at its rich, burnished luster
Summoning up all the willpower I could muster
My forbearance was soon overcome
By joyous supplications
As she urged me to forget any calorie calculations
And indulge in this nourishment

Relaxing further into the cushioned seat
I listened to her animated chatter
As she pointed out in the passing scenery
All the things I had forgotten that really mattered
The perfect harmony
Of nature in all its splendor and fury
"Can you not see Her signs?" she queried

Slowly, I began to enjoy this freedom
Of not having to agonize and reason
And trust instead in little me's magical imagination
The creative intuition
That she would find the way through
The breathtaking views

But soon enough, I found myself ruminating
About all that needed to be done tomorrow
And all that had been missed out on yesterday
Constricting me with fear
The veils of doubt began once again obscuring the atmosphere

"Wake up, Mama!"
My son's excited breath tickles my ear
It is 5am, and the weekend
"What time are we going to the ice cream shop today?"
Seeing his angelic face, my terrors disentangle
As I giggle and cuddle
"You are the boss!"

# THE UNOPENED GIFT

Inside her there is an
Abandoned
Dependent
Wounded
Child

Living in
Self-pity and isolation
Unworthiness and depression
Needing validation
Looking back and haunted by "if onlys"
Nurturing the wound with
"Why does this always happen to me?"

But what she really fears is change
Of flexing her emotional range
That would obliterate the victim role
And her belief that she was born broken
Not coming into this world whole

The solution is simple
It is in fact child's play
Of taking the shadows and making from them colorful papier mâchés
With imaginative curiosity
And joyous creativity

Because inside her there is also a
Magical
Innocent
Child

That little one dances in present time
Moving easily between this dimension and others
With genuine conviction
That her tales are not fiction

Uninhibited in her feelings
She is not stuck in a single identity
But flows with ease instead
From an emotion and character to the next
Trusting
That all is as it should be

The playful one knows that within her there is also an
Eternal
Divine
Child

The first spark that created her
Lies buried still in her heart
All it needs is but a dab
Of her mystical scepter
To envision that she is indeed a reflector
Of Loveliness

There is no need to resist
This precious gift
Is it not now time to gleefully open it?

# CIRCLES AND TRIANGLES

In the playground of life
There are merry-go-rounds and slides
That can make for quite a joyride
If you keep an open heart and mind
To the circles and triangles

Like three rest stops on a long road
Emancipating. Eating. Examining
From rejecting the diet mentality
And respecting and becoming present in your body
To honoring your hunger
And feeding your needs underneath of
All the fears, limiting beliefs, and meanings

Flooding with
the awareness that these
Are but spokes in a wheel
Going from the rim to the hub
Where resides a nurturing Mother
The single center supporting the whole
Remembering also that although their stings
May cause painful emotions
Without each radius in the sphere
There can be no motion

In the family constellation, too,
These universal shapes appear
Starting with two and then becoming three
Child, in-law, parent, sibling, or spouse
Creating hierarchies
And conflicting loyalties
With power struggles between the superior and inferior
Or instead, egalitarian networks
Where everyone shares and takes responsibility
Joining hands in a circumference
Not of manipulation but benevolence

Perhaps you are a misfit
Leaving your household feeling overwhelmed
Deeply sensitive and intuitive
Finding your sweet spot in solitude
Rather than standing in the spotlight
Where you fear your thin skin
Would be set alight
Wanting to be the observer rather than a participant
Repeatedly told: "Come out of your shell!"
Believing that something within you is not right
So that you plunge into food obsessions
A circle trying to fit into a world of triangles

You may think you are separate
Far away from kindred
But therein lies the paradox
The cause of your suffering
As you remain trapped in your mind and ego

Because you are not apart, but a part
Of the Whole
Circle and triangle, both
On the journey
Yet already Home

# TASTY TREAT

## IT'S A BREEZE BUTTERCUP'S PEAS

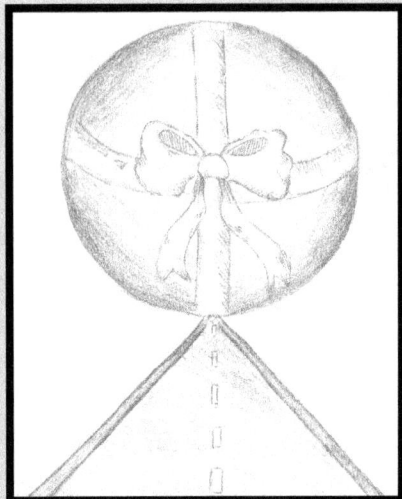

1 kilo frozen peas

1½-inch fresh ginger cut into thin rounds

1 handful of chopped green coriander

4 green chilies

Lemon juice

*Chaat masala* (a ready-made blend of spices available in many grocery stores)

Salt to taste

Oil

1. Boil the peas in 1½ liters of water, making sure they are not overdone.

2. Drain water and set the peas aside.

3. In a large pan, add 2 tablespoons of oil and fry the ginger until it is light brown. Then add the green chilies and fry for a minute.

4. Throw in half the peas with some salt and fry. Also add half the chopped coriander. Stir in a folding movement.

5. Add the rest of the peas and the remaining coriander. Check for salt and add as required.

Serve with juicy slices of lemon and sprinkled *chaat masala*.

"THIS ANTECHAMBER
IS BUT A VESTIBULE
FOR GROWTH
AND BECOMING..."

# DRINKS

# SWEET GENES

There is a trump card for my compulsive overeating
That I have sometimes used to justify its continuing
The fact that I am a direct descendant
Of a 12th century Sufi mystic
Hazrat Baba Farid Masood Ganjshakar

His bestowed name is the key
To explain away my helplessness when faced with sugary treats
Because my great, great...grandfather
Had been named by his master
"The Treasury of Sweetness" or Ganjshakar

There are several legends that surround
The granting of this designation
Starting from my venerable ancestor's childhood
When his mother, to awaken him
For early morning worship
Placed a bag of sugar under his prayer mat
For encouragement
Until one day she forgot
Yet it miraculously appeared anyhow

And then later, once he began his transformative initiations
To become the spiritual leader
Of the Chishti Order's lineage
Stories around sugar became a part of the folklore
Permeating his being, both exterior and interior

Thus, when weakened after many days of fasting
Baba Farid slipped and fell
But the mud that entered his mouth
Turned into sticky caramel
And again later, after abstaining continuously from food
Time came for nourishment
But he had nothing to fill his fiery stomach
So, he devoured some small stones
Which instantly metamorphosed into sucrose

There is yet another tale
Of a trader who foolishly said to the saint
That his bags of sugar contained salt instead
Only to find that his lie had materialized
But after a contrite confession
Baba Farid rectified the situation, saying
"If it was sugar, then let it be so!"

My forefather's humble nature was also saccharine
Daily providing sustenance for the poor and those in need
He had compassion for all
Without a care for caste nor creed
A message that was heard by Ibn Battuta and Guru Nanak Dev
And still, eight hundred years later
Thousands of devotees come on their spiritual expeditions
To his mausoleum in the city of Pakpattan

His mystical poetry also speaks
Of honeyed nectar
Cleaving lover to the Beloved
Like a little boy to his mother
Mindful of the Creator's all-encompassing company
In his verse he yearned for Unity
And many affirm that he was to Punjabi literature
A Chaucer

Like my great-times manifold grandfather
I have also been journeying
Through internal landscapes
Searching for wholeness
Longing for something
Which stood patiently waiting
At the edge of my consciousness
And imperceptibly
By blood too began to sing
On my path back Home

But in the meanwhile
I crammed my mouth with mud and stones
These psychological toxins weighed me down
And I lost sight of who I really was
But as Baba Farid enlightens
Burdens provide the foundation
For the house of equanimity

So, my penchant for date cake
With lashing of cream
Is in my genes
But I also pray for
Inclusivity and empathy
And with humble sentiment
For a sweetened writing instrument

# FOUR

The father we share
Is the bracket
Around my three sisters and I
Although it is decades since I was in his care

So, it is a household of strangers that welcomes me
When I return to the place once familiar
I confess, with some anxiety
After an absence of 30 years

3+1=4
Sky, air, earth, water
Darkness, first light, day break, sunrise
Birth, growth, knowledge, death
Falling, rising, falling, rising again
The four chambers of the heart
Create a Whole

My sisters and I know nothing
Of each other's twilights and dawns
Nor where we have arisen from our falls
Only to stumble again
And advance with a deeper comprehension

As the four elements sustain
Our Autobiography
Will we nourish each other tenderly?
To bandage the crevices
With Wholeheartedness

# 25 YEARS

She is told he is unwell
With a withering outer shell
And it is time for her to come back
After 25 years

They are two strangers with the same blood
Created with similar features from mud
But living in separate spheres

At first, abandonment blocks her path
Followed by hurt, resentment, and wrath
As that little girl he left behind reappears

She snuggles alone, hardening her soul
Forgetting that she is already whole
While the years stream past full of tears

There are so many times in the twists and turns of life
She wishes she could call upon him for support and advice
But only deafening silence fills her ears

When the appeal arrives, she is not entirely surprised
That the petitioner may want to apologize
Facing his own mortality and filled with fears

She decides to accept the invitation
"I am worth loving," is her healing incantation
And the hesitancy to step into the unknown disappears

The little girl and the middle-aged woman walk hand in hand
As they begin to understand
That wisdom is not processed in the mind, it is experienced in the heart
That is the real art
The doorway through which self-compassion premiers

Although this purification of her tyrannical parts
Requires much awareness, patience, and heart
Whenever any negative traits raise their heads and sneer

So, what happened in the last 25 years
Or will happen 25 years hence
Is of no matter
What flourishes within her today is the only barometer

# MINDFULLY PLAYING THE BLAME GAME

Sometimes there are key moments from childhood and later
That become our adult identity shapers
These experiences can leave us painfully branded
And in our restrictive stories and self-limiting beliefs stranded
Like cattle in a herd, we trudge through life
Unquestioning and interned

One such tale that kept me trapped for many years
Was the lack of any relationship with my father
Who remained silent and unobserved

And so I blamed my father for ...

Not being a cheerleader in my darkest hours
For my feelings of abandonment and rejection
Not giving me any guidance nor protection
For my lack of confidence and trust
So that I built up towering, protective walls
To make sure I would not get hurt
On this protracted disengaging
I also blamed my compulsive overeating

I craved comfort and acknowledgment
But instead got lingering indifference
So, I recreated those moods through food
My crunchy nut cornflakes never disappointed
As I focused on my belly that was full to bursting
Instead of my heart, stuffed from hurting

My internal cry grew visible on my body
And the container stretched to accommodate
But of this constant companion I began to grow weary
Suffocated by my autobiography
Rather than self-medicate I needed to self-liberate

I began to wonder, what if I blamed mindfully instead?
Focusing on all the gifts this journey had delivered

And so, I blamed my father for ...

My striving to learn and burgeon in search of my authentic self
My gentleness, sensitivity, and empathy
My unrestrained devotion to my own children that will resound through generations
My desire to help others to heal and find inspiration
My expanded consciousness
Opening the doors to true heart-full-ness

No doubt my father, too, had his reasons to stay away
He may even blame himself for this negligence
Perhaps he was unknowingly repeating patterns of his ancestry
And I was not there when he needed me

It is movement and toil that yield a good harvest
Otherwise, the earth remains hardened
And the treasures underneath seeking manifestation stay hidden
Philosophers affirm that pain lifts the veil of forgetfulness
And that we thirst for something even closer than a father or a mother
To satiate us with the kind of Love no mortal can deliver
So, to my father I am grateful for being this instrument of divine favor

## SUNRISE

Today, she has the choice of tolerating
A stroll along a challenging pathway
Where the abandoned child within her rages
Without delay
And stomps her angry, little feet
Screaming with fury until her lungs become weak
As her adult self looks on
Compassionately
Encircling the little one within
In love

A youngster cares nothing for kismet
Nor that those around her have their own reasons
For any difficult determinations
Even though these may shake her very foundations
And leave her feeling terrified and desolate
Short-changed of her birth right

So, it is not easy
When her grown up part is called upon to play happy families
Expected to forget decades of neglect
Like it was all a bad dream
And that of what was her due
She was robbed
Left in the darkness to sob

That lonely little girl had given herself many treats
Of zinging chili chips, orange ice lollies, and gooey sweetmeats
Waiting for absent guardians to call
It was like rubbing into a deep lesion biting alcohol
While crossing off the days until the next visit
On a calendar on the wall

But just as her mature part had been
On a remedial journey of the mind
The small child needed some space
To find a secure and welcoming resting place
In the heart
And be adored like a treasure
Beyond measure
The wise ones tell us that
Light enters through the wound
But healing from heartache
Requires that we become attuned
To a subtle frequency
That first unlocks the heavy gates
Of our pulsating piths
Tenderly
To let the Radiance in
Otherwise, we just remain a victim
Frozen
In a casket of self-pity
Unchanged

And in this transformed dimension
While the incensed child feels safe to vent
Her ripened constituent
Can reach out with a soft heart
To the absconder
Beholding with empathy their hurt half-pint
And move towards a fresh start
On a trajectory all together
To create authentic moments
And rejoice in the
Sunrise

# LEGACY

Some say that the compulsion for binging
Can be passed on from mother to offspring
But in my case
There was never a trace
Of maternal guzzlings
If anything, my disposition was to my mother a conundrum
Most puzzling

Perhaps it was something in my genetic makeup
As there were members of my wider family
Who were in both the over and under deregulated eating
Habit ensnared
So, while well meaning
Mum put me on my first diet at age 10

My daughter, having recently surpassed this birthday
Is already showing the signs of
Being trapped in a poor body image cage
She is moving into the comparisons, self-consciousness, and hiding phase
Telling me that she would be happier
If only a few kilos lighter
Emphatic in the dislike of her shape

Her words fill me with dismay
And I am transported back to my formative teenage stint
Spent in Tokyo with expat parents
Where everyone looked hopelessly "perfect"
And I stole money from my mother's purse
To feed my growing hankerings
Filled with confusion and remorse
For research confirming that early dieting often leads to early obesity
I would in time become the cover girl
But this was one torch
Of which I was NOT about to let my daughter take charge

Unfortunately, she had already witnessed
My many years of calorie counting, dieting, and over exercise chaos
And the impact of my erratic behaviors and practices on her was implicit
As she told me without hesitation: "Mama, I am fat."
And disliked all her body parts
So, I was determined that my weight watching past
Would not become her obsessive future
There would be no room in our home
For co-dependent dieting
We chatted about the dangers of food restriction
Especially in the adolescent years
Triggering biological, physical, and psychological afflictions
And that her body's evolution
Coupled with often uncontrollable internal commotion
Were perfectly normal
Helping her to take up the challenge
Of her rite of passage

Moving towards body acceptance and respect
We tried to decipher which of her needs were unmet
With positive affirmations and lists of her strengths
To put down the foundations
For a lasting, healthy relationship with her self

From this framework we are trying to ascend
To the more complex realm of food independence
Relying on moderation not willpower
Honoring and trusting her hunger and fullness signals
With kind-heartedness
Authorizing all foods
Focusing on creating a happy mood
And a balanced attitude

Through my daughter's journey
Although it is by no means easy
I have been given such a precious gift
Of clearing my own childhood mists
To discover a truth that has always been present
That within us both resides a Wise Woman
Waiting to be awakened

# TASTY TREAT   ## ENJOY TODAY WITH A FRUIT COCKTAIL

1 cup orange juice

1 cup grapefruit juice

1 cup pineapple juice

2 apples, peeled and grated

1 cup mango pulp

3-4 cans of cream soda or lemonade

1 small bunch mint (optional)

Ice cubes

1.  Combine the grated apples with the mango pulp and set aside.
2.  In a large bowl or jug, mix all the juices.
3.  Before serving, combine the above two and add the cans of cream soda or lemonade along with some ice cubes.
4.  Fresh mint leaves may be added, if so desired.

"WITHIN US
RESIDES
A WISE WOMAN
WAITING TO BE
AWAKENED"

# DESSERTS AND INFUSION

# CHASING CROCODILES

Recounting the happenings of his school day, my young son illuminates
"Mama, we learnt about Steve Irwin. He taught people about wildlife and died at age 44. Now he is in heaven, chasing crocodiles!"
"Chasing crocodiles?"
"Well of course Mama, he was the Crocodile Hunter."
My son looks at me with indulgence
As if the reason is self-evident, which he then states
"When you go back up, you forget everything, except what you love."

To walk the path of doing what you love may not be easy
Saddled as you might be with so many responsibilities
But unless you do what you need to feel complete
Your soul will wither like forget-me-nots in the heat
And you will have nothing left to transport
Back to Eternity Resort

So, while on Earth, why not:

**F**ollow an activity with clear goals, balancing challenge and skill, paying attention to your evolution
**L**ose yourself in the sweet spot of effortlessly engaging fully in the moment
**O**utside time, feel the hours fly by like minutes as all self-consciousness evaporates and you become part of a greater Presence
**W**ith a sense of control, despite the risk of failure, become passionately immersed

In essence, embody Steve Irwin and be in FLOW

So, chase your crocodiles
And let them chase you, too
Because as the sages caution
Don't let your throat constrict with fear
Breathe and dance in jubilation
The end hovers ever-present in the atmosphere

# OPPORTUNITIES

"Mama, do you know what an opportunity milkshake is?"
I look at my little one, tickled
And feel there are words of wisdom about to be declared
"No sweetheart. Tell me about it."
"Well, you don't always know when an opportunity is coming, or when it has gone;
only when it is happening."
A deepening of the present moment, of course
His simple message is eye-opening
"So, you drink a milkshake," he continues, "and say what you want."
Hmmm, I wonder
Like, "I want to publish a poetry book?"
"Sure!" he flashes his angelic smile
Or in other words: Set your intention
By his train of thought, I am beguiled
"And then you wait and see. Because life is hard, and it is easy."
With his final conclusion, I am left giddy

**O**penings of
**P**ossibilities and
**P**robabilities
**O**ptions and the odds in a
**R**oom full of
**T**urning points
**U**ncertainties
**N**ot grand plans
**I**n
**T**he hopeful prayers for
**Y**our lucky chance

**M**ix up
**I**ngredients
**L**inkages and juxtapositions
**K**nead
**S**ynthesize
**H**ave a purpose
**A**malgamate
**K**eep your fingers crossed
**E**mptying

# THE LEGEND OF THE MILLIPEDE RUNNER

"God did not make any mechanical device for time. He made an animal – called the Millipede Runner. Have you heard its legend?" queries my young son one fine morning
I feel a story coming on and ask for more

"It lives deep inside the Earth, Mama. There is one in every planet, so there are millions of them."
"How interesting. And what does it do?" I encourage
"Well Mama, as it runs, time runs. If it stops, time stops. They can start and stop, like cars."
"That's wonderful sweetie, and why would they stop?"
"If there is something blocking them of course! They have really strong, small white horns, to push all the mud and stones out of the way. They run at medium speed on all their tiny legs, not too fast and not too slow. Otherwise every minute would be like one hour, or everything would finish too quickly!"
His logic makes sense, and I join in his chuckling

"Oh, and they come in many colors. Like green, black, orange, and pink," he continues
"Is this a story you heard in school?" I ask bemused
"Nooooo!"
He does not of my doubting approve
"You see Mama, I just remembered it."
But to allay my suspicions
I do a quick Google inspection
And concede that in my distrust I was mistaken

The image my son conjures up is enchanting
Of a determined, colorful creature with luminescent antlers
Burning through darkened space
Like a flickering candle flame

I begin to wonder
What if each of us is a millipede runner?
Journeying through life with tunnel vision
Until a large boulder brings to a screeching halt our expedition
And time seems frozen
Like hitting rock bottom in an inky ocean

Are we able to tolerate these birth pangs?
As Mary did, gasping against the trunk of that palm tree
Pushing through the sweet, sharp pain of her yearning
Surrendering
Delivering a transformed self and a new reality
There is a toll for our resistance
Because whether we like it or not
That hard stone will at some point be obstructing our path
And if we freeze in fear and worry
Time will become heavy
Like an elastic band we will feel pulled taut
Constantly vibrating with low energy

But if we choose to be present at that surrender point
Trusting that we do possess the tenacity
To excavate through not a hurdle but an opportunity
Like mini-Earths in the deep ground of Being
To discover our soul piece by piece
Time will start to run again

# TASTY TREAT

## BABA FARID'S SWEET DELIGHT

500 grams rice

250 grams *chana dal* (split chickpeas)

1/2 teaspoon baking powder

1 liter warmed milk

500 grams sugar

2 full tbsp clarified butter (*ghee*)

8 green cardamoms

A pinch of saffron, dissolved in 1 tsp milk (optional)

A few drops rose water (optional)

1. Thoroughly wash the *dal* and rice separately. The *channa dal* should be soaked in 4 cups of water overnight with half a teaspoon of baking powder. Then throw away the overnight water and add 3 cups of fresh water. Put it in a pot and place on fire. After a first boil of the *dal* on high heat, remove the white foam that accumulates on the surface and continue to simmer it partly covered on low heat until it is half-cooked. This can take at least half an hour and the water should then be mostly evaporated.

2. The rice should be soaked for a minimum of an hour, and then drained to be added to the half-cooked split chickpeas.

3. Pour in 1 liter of warmed milk to the above, cover and steam on low heat till the *dal* and rice grains are tender, and all the milk is fully absorbed. Stir occasionally to make sure the mixture does not get burnt at the bottom.

4. Now add the sugar and cover and cook on low heat for about ten minutes or until totally dissolved.

5. Take seeds from the cardamom pods and crush in a pestle and mortar to release their flavor.

6. Put the *ghee* in a small pan and melt it on a low flame. Add the cardamom seeds and fry for half a minute. Then pour this mixture on the rice and split chickpea pudding and stir thoroughly.

Serve slightly warmed. Another variation is to skip on the *ghee* and simply add saffron and rose water instead of the crushed cardamoms. This dish has the right amount of sweet for Faridis but may pack too high a sugar punch for some. Therefore, reduce the sugar to your taste!

# INFUSION

## CINNAMON SPICE TEA

A pinch (1/8 teaspoon) each of:
    cinnamon
    nutmeg
    dry ginger powders

1 teaspoon green tea leaves

500 ml (about 2 cups) boiling water

Organic honey to taste

Add the tea leaves and powders to a teapot and pour in the boiling water. Brew for three minutes. Strain and mix in the organic honey.

# MENU THREE

## IT'S NOT YOU

# A NOTE FROM THE CHEF

Food has all kinds of meanings that have nothing to do with satisfying physical hunger, which I have tried to explore in the two preceding Menus. And I must confess that providing pathways for the reader through my poems, that were birthed more in my unconscious than conscious mind without any particular road map, has had me throwing my arms up in exasperation at times. It was after such a late-night moment, when the next day out of the blue, my young son chirped up from the back seat of the car as he buckled his seatbelt. "Mama," he intoned, "I have to tell you something." My mind distracted with to-do lists, I frankly was not paying much attention. "Mama, I have an idea for a poem for you," he continued. And here is what he said:

"Buckle up and get ready for the best journey of your life.

Called: The 5 most important things in the world according to a 6 year old, in no particular order:

1. Love
2. Believing in God
3. Believing in heaven
4. Believing in angels
5. Safety

You have now reached your destination."

I sat there stunned, humbled yet again by a sign from beyond, affirming that through Grace I had gained strength. So, too, now, I was being called upon to trust the process. It was also a reminder that apart from the self-love and shelter I found by listening to my physical and emotional forms,

soul satisfaction was revealed in the inward journey in pursuit of the formless.

The path of awakening from the limited consciousness of fear, conditioning, and compulsion to the expansive awareness of divine consciousness is, of course, a very personal journey. It has been said that there are as many routes to God as there are seekers, and each adventure is unique.

As I mentioned earlier, I have gravitated towards Sufism, which is a mystical path of love in which God (or Truth) is experienced as the Beloved. It resonated within my heart because for many years I felt like an exile longing for completion. I sought to fill the emptiness within by external means, such as dieting, binging, etc., believing that "you are what you weigh," but still ending up disappointed even once my goal weight was reached. This can be described as the journey from God, in which I felt like a child, alone, lost and hungry, trapped in the illusions of the stories and beliefs of the ego.

However, in the depths of my compulsion and despair, through the spark of Grace, the soul's memory of satiety and surrender ignited the fire of longing and belonging. Over time, guides appeared, both in written and human guise, pointing out that it was the transformation of my heart that I sought, as much as that of my body and eating psychology. I was now on the journey to God. Thus, a more non-judgmental observer materialized, along with new, emerging beliefs around my relationship with food and the burgeoning of a more intimate relationship with the Beloved.

In this growing love affair, moving away from the duality of separation towards Oneness, my heart naturally expanded with self-acceptance and love, although the doubts and confusions of the mind continued to haunt me.

The final segment of this odyssey encompasses the journey in God. In this context, it would be where food no longer needs to be the pathway, because it has stepped aside and instead, the heart is in complete alignment with Presence, without effort nor will, united with the Eternal — dissolving like golden honey in warmed water. Few achieve this exalted station, and I am certainly far from it as I continue my humble wayfaring to God.

In this final Menu, I explore healing through Wholeness on my quest towards the Beloved, with the realization that we are all individualized Spirit. These poems are the beginning of an integration and a melting away of boundaries from my false self into the essential Self. Indeed, most of what appears here was written in a receptive, quiet state, with my mind and heart holding focus with intention and yet open to receive.

In *It's Not You*, I am reminded that my hand is commanded by the Invisible, pouring forth a words binge catalyzing my unfolding, as I sit at the *Crossroads* between craving and fulfillment. Traveling through a dark *Labyrinth* of obsessions and self-loathing, I follow the thread of my longing back to the Light. But there are many dark nights along the way, and I take heed not to go too *Fast*. I persevere between the *Parallel Lines* of fear and growth, looking upon the Beloved with my *Love Face*. And there I create a sacred *S.P.A.C.E.* to inhabit not only my own body and emotions but the whole Universe all at once. As an *Emblem* of the Infinite in this boundless expanse, I begin to awaken as if from an interminable sleep to recall that I am *A Beautiful Poem*.

Once the sweetness of freedom is tasted, it never leaves. However, I do forget it at times and fall back into my compulsive eating. It is still one step forwards, two backwards, so I *Mind*

*the Gap* between thought and first bite, feeling unworthy and being sacred. As I explore in *Hey, Rumi*, even the sages sometimes stumble across the gap, because like us all they, too, are human beings trying to find their way back Home. But of course, a wise teacher is much further along the pilgrimage into the inner world than a novice student, for whom the most difficult part is in the *Knowing and Unknowing*, allowing herself to know what she has always known — that this wandering is but a circumnavigation back to Herself.

However, this is not about just identifying with the spiritual quest without putting in the hard, sometimes difficult work of overcoming what may be at the core of emotional eating, or any other urges. It means allowing in that wounded, terrified child who may be rejected and abandoned, banging on the door and wanting to be let in and comforted. I have already explored this in the Main Courses section of the previous Menu, but here I want to underline that the energetic movements of emotions that come up are tolerated and released with the help of resources.

Thus, as the clouds gathered and in the pouring rain, I held in my heart those loved ones no longer sheathed in their biology. My grandfather (*Nana*), grandmother (*Nani*) and nature (symbolized in *The Bougainvillea Tree*) were my constant, patient companions as I sat with the fragmented parts of my undigested pain, while they refused to allow me to abandon myself. As I explored the relationship with my treasured, departed step-father in *Treadmill Grieving* and *Butterfly*, he, too, came to join this supportive circle.

Accordingly, I traveled with inquisitiveness through a patchwork of perplexities, towards a far horizon bathed in *Luminosity*. My path brightened by *The Light of Moses*, I dug into the rich earth of my emotions, coming up with sparkling *Gem Bones*. In *Recycling*, I am reminded that sometimes we need to be broken open to be made whole, as we humbly surrender to the freedom of being *Dieless*. Thus ends *Today's Lesson* in gratitude and awe.

# STARTERS

# IT'S NOT YOU

On the way home in the car one evening
My young son and I sit quietly, daydreaming
When his pensive voice wafts across from the back seat
"Mama, are you still writing poetry?"

After my confirmation
He then proceeds with this elucidation:
"Mama, you did not think of these things. God thought of these poems.
Then He gave the ideas to you. The people will think they are yours,
but actually, they are not. It's not you."

It is as if he has read my mind
It is true that when I sit with pen in hand
I do set my intention to compose from the heart
Imploring the Beloved to illuminate my path

Because I struggle often with articulating
My haphazard musings
Feeling like there is precious treasure
Buried just beyond the reach of my endeavors

And then a quiet voice within inspires:
"You will get there eventually. But first you need more seasoning,
to plunge into the Root of your art and out of mental reasoning."
I need to let the knowledge from enlightened guides
Percolate into my heart and therein comfortably reside
As I am clarified, fortified, mystified, and unified
Patiently doing my homework by the Light
And in its warmth continue to write

This is a forever journey taken at leisure
Unfolding has no "sell by" measure
The key is to become conscious
That there is neither arrival nor departure
For the divine spark is already within each traveler

Feeding you these scribblings
Is my privilege and reward
My service to the sacred scintilla encased in your human frame
Also provides me with the opportunity of remembering
And for my soul is deeply nourishing

So, I hope you will stay a while
And take your time to enjoy this feast
Indulge each spoonful as the heartfelt gift it is meant to be
Both from myself and the One Reality
To set you free

# CROSSROADS

Dear God, what is this lunacy!
Me, writing poetry?
Give me a juicy essay, or a short story
Plot, setting, character
Conflict, theme, narrator
But the elements of verse?
It feels like a different cosmos

I don't want to deliberate
Over the key ingredients of these couplets
Instead, I crave the freedom
To create without rhyme nor reason

These poems will not only be a path back to my own sovereignty
To break the spell of helplessness and melancholy
But also, I hope, open for others a window
To breathe and know they are not alone

Through these phrases I will find my own form
As they feed my emotional hunger
In a way food never could
From compulsive eating to compulsive writing
A words binge catalyzing my unfolding

They will force me to be in the present moment
Becoming an empty vessel ready for possibilities
Giving attention to my challenges and capabilities
A poet searching for her Poem
As I pass through the shadowlands into Light

At the crossroads between the "i" and "I"
While I become a witness to my own life
And also something bigger
This is my Remembering

It is written that She gives according to need
So, I must trust that the ideas will flow
As my craft I continue to varnish
And while the inner world begins to radiate with clarity
The outer, too, will reflect those heartfelt qualities
With each poem the path will appear
Like one of my son's magic picture books
I will polish the mirror of my heart
Because that is my appointed task
And so I proceed on this journey, with humility

# LABYRINTH

As a young girl
I did not think I was a part of this world
But rather, a bodiless ghost
With a distended head that played host
To vast quantities of provisions

But no matter how much I stuffed my face
The emptiness remained, unchanged
And my self-loathing grew
With yet another dieting attempt not followed through

I was convinced I had a character defect
Making it impossible for me to be treasured
Held, guided, or remembered
Even by the Creator Herself

Instead of examining what was actually going on
I focused only on things I was doing wrong
Quick to convict without a trial
I was judge, jury, and executioner
Feeling ashamed to be so out of control
And totally lacking in willpower

As far as I was concerned
All rational thoughts and behaviors around eating had adjourned
Evidence that I was damaged
Needing to be desperately repackaged

It was a painful and lonely labyrinth
Without beginning nor end
And food was my chosen companion
Both embraced and despised
Bringing me to my knees
In this safe, tiny space I survived for years
Unwilling to face my needs, inner appetites, and fears

Until from deep within a soft lament arose:
"I have been trying to awaken you, my dearest
Take my Light and burn away the veils of separation
They are but an illusion
Follow the thread of your longing back to Me
Into the Unknown."

And the heavy bolts to a door in the labyrinth unfastened

# TASTY TREAT    ## VITALITY RECOUP BUTTERNUT SQUASH SOUP

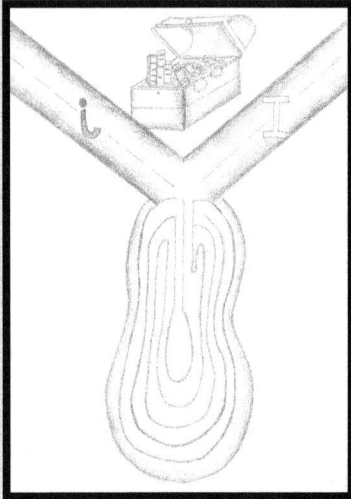

2 carrots

1 medium sweet potato

1 medium butternut squash

1 medium leek

1-inch ginger, peeled

4 cloves garlic, peeled

2 tablespoons butter

2 vegetable stock cubes

5 black peppercorns

1-inch cinnamon stick

2 bay leaves

2 tablespoons olive oil

1. Peel and chop the carrots, sweet potato and butternut squash into medium-sized pieces.

2. Combine the diced vegetables with the black peppercorns, garlic, ginger and cinnamon, bringing to a boil over medium heat in about 5 cups of water before simmering for 20 minutes.

3. Now dice and add the leeks, boiling for a further 10 minutes or until soft.

4. Transfer cooked vegetables with some of the water (minus the cinnamon stick) to a food processor and whiz to a smooth puree.

5. In a large pan, heat 2 tablespoons of olive oil over a medium heat and add the butter, vegetable stock cubes, and bay leaves — stir for a few minutes.

6. Add the pureed vegetables to the heated oil and simmer on low heat for 5 minutes.

Enjoy this silky soup with crackers or ciabatta bread.

# "WHAT IF EACH OF US IS A MILLIPEDE RUNNER?"

# MAIN COURSES

# FAST

The velocity of living
Can seem unforgiving
With countless enumerations
We become engorged

In the self-indulgent fire
Of our frivolous desires
We are seduced by
Wanton entertainment

Absorbed with the directions
But what is the intention
Of this expectation?

To anchor steadfast into earth
And nurture not the branch but the roots
Thirsting for the indissoluble
And everlasting

One path to this embodiment
Is paradoxically abandonment
Of sustenance, to weaken the
Impatient ego

As the withholding of both what enters and exits
Food, harmful speech, and activity
Disrupts unconscious ideology
A holy emancipation
And a deeper remembrance replaces enslavement
As the soul focuses on the present
Savoring the sweetest
Elixir

# LOVE FACE

Many of us subsist in the narrow house of anxieties
Imagining what could happen
The possibilities of potentialities
Swirl and suffocate
In the angst of being rejected or hurt
We duck behind circumvention and procrastination

Perhaps we found refuge
Inside those safe walls
Driven in by some painful personal history
But now we have grown taller
And cannot even stand upright in it any longer

Should we annihilate
confront or embrace
Our fears?

Better to entrust them to the battlefield
To be vanquished by something mightier than our selves
To surrender and become a prisoner
To the Ultimate Conqueror
Who has the key to unlock our hearts
And deliver us from our irrational agitation

The taste of this defeat
Is ever so sweet
As we arise from the confines of our apprehensions
To breathe in instead this new-found freedom
Setting our feet firmly on the expansive
Ground of awareness
Cultivating presence

Our scared face is transmuted to a Love Face
And we pass through fear to awe

# PARALLEL LINES

Within the four walls of these poems
I feel free to be and experiment
No need to take the exit
The ideas keep flowing
Sometimes, not of my own doing

Sentences line up
One after the next
Often leaving me perplexed
With their harmonious build-up

The onward march
Along this path
Is done without fear
Of what may, or may not, be near

I plunge headlong into this journey
As the sparkling waters of creativity
Sustain me
I am
Light-minded
Light-hearted

Oh, how I wish I could transmit
That same jubilation
The elation
To this worldly orbit

Where I am trapped instead by anticipatory anxiety
Of coulds, shoulds, and woulds
A sobering variety
Of daunting likelihoods

Playful with the game of writing
I am unable to trust the process of living
The two roads running in parallel
Not crisscrossing

But as the sages intimate
To desire a thing is to desire its prerequisite
So, to be forgiving has no meaning
Without some conflict first intervening

I must be patient
And believe that this, too, is a season
Of growth and integration
An adventure at once
Exasperating and
Illuminating

# S.P.A.C.E.

Sacred
Paradisiac
All-powerful
Celestial
Eternal

Soulful
Poetic
Authentic
Conscious
Essence

Serene
Present
Aligned
Centered
Embodied

Simple
Playful
Angelic
Childlike
Exploration

Self-love
Precious
Appreciative
Compassionate
Endearing

Safe
Protector
Advocate
Caretaker
Entrust

Superwoman
Proactive
Accomplished
Courageous
Empowered

Synchronicity
Possibilities
Awakening
Clarity
Eureka

# EMBLEM

11 paces from my front door
The air is satiated
With the luscious scent of delicate white flowers
Their botanical name: Jasminum sambac "Grand Duke of Tuscany"

The fragrance tickles my soul
With a restlessness
A longing for something
That will unlock my sight
To a more profound authenticity

Which is filled with the whisperings of:
You can trust yourself
You are worthy
You are a cherished flower

This hunger within
Can no longer be appeased with
The dull taste of chocolate
Nor the monotonous crunch of grub

A prison of flesh and blood
The claustrophobic walls are disfigured
By my heartless touch
As the wounds fester

Why can I not be like the jasmine flower?
Flourishing in the scorching warmth of
The passionate sun
An exquisite burgeoning

Perhaps the affliction is itself the blessing
Opening up my senses
And the discomfort a necessity
Just as the heat transforms dormant buds
Into emblems of the Infinite

It is time to unbolt the doors of this house
Allowing the cloying aroma
To permeate inwards
And feel blessed in each moment of
Being broken open
The incandescence in this reality
Is the key that unlocks the gate
To the innermost divine temple

Expanding from the outside in
Appears paradoxical
Yet therein lies another face of Truth
Of the All-Seeing, All-Hearing, All-Aware, the Nourisher

Why not then radiate this heavenly perfume?
From my miniature jasmine tree within
To all whom I meet
No matter if their homes are darkened and padlocked
Remembering that deep inside their heartlands, too
Are embryonic Grand Dukes, restless and yearning

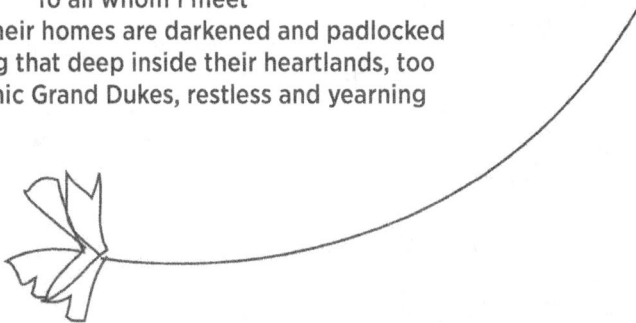

# A BEAUTIFUL POEM

Perhaps you live
In the fortress of judgment
With shame, regret, anger, and blame
Bullying, bickering, brutalizing
Shouting ultimatums
To a deepening separateness, a haven

Yet, just beyond the impenetrable encirclement
Is a verdant resting place
Of tall palm trees laden with juicy dates
And weeping willows caressing the waters
Of a mirror-like lake

One is the house of unconscious compulsion
The other a space of conscious awareness
One the abode of the self-critical observee
The other an arena of the non-judgmental observer

Why not be adventurous and throw open a window
Or better still, invite the eyewitness in
Perhaps she could teach you a thing or two
And unlock vistas you have never seen

A tête-à-tête over a hearty meal would be ideal
As you take your places by a warm fire
Don't hesitate to explore your heart's desires
Keep an open mind and liberally communicate
With the key phrase: "How fascinating!"

Notice how she
Asks. Waits. Listens
Without admonition
How she brings attention to your emotions
Which serve the function of a calming mechanism
And to your bodily sensations
"Am I hungry? What am I feeling?"
To your thought patterns, too
Around dieting and your body's indent
Where so much of your time and energy is spent

She will lead you to a secret place
Through a winding, darkened tunnel
A room in your citadel where the glimmer
May still be subtle
Of compassion and grace

And as you stay present
In this boundless expanse
You will begin to awaken from an interminable sleep
Gradually becoming mindful of when, how, and where you eat
But without chastisement
And with the choice
Of turning off the autopilot switch

Walking out of habit and into comprehension
Out of defensiveness into curiosity
But, at first, without changing a thing
Because that will whip you right back
Into the diet trap
Without exploring the triggers

This softness of stillness and breathing
Gently watching
Is the place of Remembering
Of accepting, learning, and growing
Of returning

Until finally on the pink rose and lavender walls of that room
There will appear a mirror
And the face in it, for the moment
Will be your own
But as you seek out more clues
The Truth behind it will slowly shine through

The hook of Love will then be in your throat
Draining your illusions
Reeling you in
Indeed, the Beloved is closer to you than your jugular vein

And as you continue to stare
You will become aware
That you are a beautiful poem
Composed by the Object in full view

# TASTY TREAT

## SMOKED SALMON WITH CREAM CHEESE PARCEL

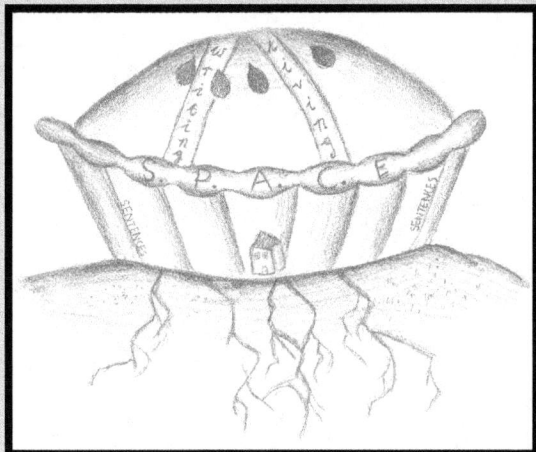

1 box of Philadelphia cream cheese with garlic and herbs

200 grams smoked salmon

1 egg yolk

2 sheets of rolled, puff pastry

1. Preheat oven to 220 degrees Celsius.
2. Take a sheet of puff pastry and roll it to the size of your baking dish (medium sized preferable).
3. Spread out well all the contents of the cream cheese over the pastry sheet, making sure to leave about a 1-centimeter gap all around the edge.
4. Cover the cream cheese in strips of smoked salmon (again making sure to leave the 1 cm gap).
5. Wet the edges of the pastry sheet with some water and cover the salmon and cheese with the second sheet. Pinch both pastry sheets together to seal properly the contents of the parcel.
6. Brush all over with the egg yolk.
7. Bake in the preheated oven for 30 minutes.

This dish is delicious served hot with a simple salad.

If you have leftover salmon:

1. Put the smoked salmon on a flat dish, cover with a bit of olive oil.
2. Sprinkle with pink peppercorns and finely chopped fresh dill.
3. Serve with toasted bread.

# SIDE DISHES

# MIND THE GAP

Mind the gap between:

strategy and action
victim and warrior
event and interpretation
instruction manual and undergoing
permanency and risk taking
narrow vision and big picture
part and whole
isolation and contribution
fragmentation and integration
self and selves
learning and unlearning
resistance and acceptance
loathing and compassion
crawling and flying
worst enemy and best friend
unworthy and sacred
masks and vulnerability
cravings and satisfaction
want and need
physical hunger and emotional hunger
thought and first bite
animal and angel
mind and heart
healthy body and healthy soul
outer and inner
analysis and beingness

wandering and standing still
suffering and surrender
illusion and truth
traveling and coming home
fear and trust
holding on and letting go
slumber and awakening
forgetting and remembering
hindrance and opening
understanding and mystery
reasoning and intuition
a drop and the ocean
birth and death
sage and child
ordinary and extraordinary
coincidence and synchronicity
disregard and gratitude
static and attunement
absence and presence
visible and invisible
then and now
there and here
dark seas and a Lighthouse
self-development and alchemy
preamble and poetry

# HEY, RUMI

Hey, Rumi, I just read one of your discourses
What in the world???
Did you have a fight with your wife that morning?
So all you could spew were contemptuous warnings!

Such as, that men must endure
Our tyranny, bad character, and aggression
Our domineering attitude and oppression
Our absurdities and transgressions
Seriously?

You say that this is a battle
You wage day and night
But we pay no heed
And guided by our own foolish whims do we proceed

You advise menfolk
To endure with forbearance this yoke
And surrender to the cruelties
Of our deranged personalities

You preach that this torment refines men's characters
By fostering patience and self-control
Allowing them to come closer to their spiritual goals
As this penance absolves their own contamination
We become a source of purification

So, am I to infer
That your sublime poetry long devoured by me
Was not written for womenfolk in mind
But only those of your own kind?
And you would rather eye our silhouettes
Than partake in stimulating tête-à-têtes?

The pedestal lies fragmented
As in your petulance you vented
Diminished in dignity
I remain stunned by your ignorance of female emotional literacy

But I cannot ignore
That your quatrains have unlocked my core
And your wise words have been my mentors
As you gently took my hand
And we walked towards the Beloved

So, I choose to see you for who you are
A human, after all
Not a saint without flaws
But like the rest of us
On a journey
Trying to find your way back Home

# KNOWING AND UNKNOWING

Once you grasp, you cannot release
Once you observe, you cannot hide

Once you empathize, you cannot anesthetize
Once you comprehend, you cannot misunderstand

Once you empower, you cannot oppress
Once you appreciate, you cannot invalidate

Once you absorb, you cannot extricate
Once you embrace, you cannot hate

Once you flourish, you cannot atrophy
Once you celebrate, you cannot be melancholy

Once you honor, you cannot shame
Once you forgive, you cannot blame

Once you contribute, you cannot complain
Once you cherish, you cannot abandon

Once you acknowledge, you cannot disown
Once you alchemize, you cannot decelerate

Once you embody, you cannot disintegrate
Once you savor, you cannot forget the flavor

Once you trust, you cannot fear
Once aware, you become a mirror

Knowing that the Truth is near

# TASTY TREAT     SPINACH AND POMEGRANATE SALAD

**For the Spinach and Pomegranate Salad:**
>   100 grams spinach, carefully washed
>   1/2 large mango, peeled and chopped
>   50 grams fresh pomegranate seeds
>   2 tablespoons walnuts (optional)

**For the Dressing:**
>   3 tablespoons olive oil
>   1 tablespoon balsamic vinegar
>   Salt and freshly ground black pepper

1.  Mix together all the ingredients for the salad dressing. In a bowl, combine the spinach, mango, and fresh pomegranate seeds and toss with the dressing.
2.  Sprinkle walnuts on top (optional)

This is an easy and fresh salad, especially enjoyable during long, hot summer months.

"ONCE YOU EMBODY,
YOU CANNOT
DISINTEGRATE.
ONCE YOU SAVOR,
YOU CANNOT FORGET
THE FLAVOR"

# DRINKS

# NANA

On a bleak afternoon
More than 30 years ago today
We got the terrible news
That your soul had ascended
Reclaimed by the Beloved

Just a few days earlier
My nine-year-old heart had been feeling afraid
And my dull thoughts unable to coagulate
Until I saw you looking down at me from the landing
"Have fun at the birthday party my dear!"
I instantly knew then the reason for my deep fear
I would never see you again

There was neither rhyme nor reason
For this premonition
At 63, you were as well as could be
And traveling overseas for a conference
Always an active retiree

"Please don't go, Nana!" I pleaded
But my cries remained unheeded
And when I called home
From a noisy house in which my little friends roamed
I was told you had already left for the airport
And my breath choked

In the following days
I got busy with life, as is a child's way
But often asked the adults around me, when you would be back
As I keenly felt your lack

I have carried this empty, weathered box in my heart for so many years
But now it is filled to the brim with treasures

Of when we used to go for vanilla ice cream
As I stood behind the driver's seat
And put my chubby arms around your neck
I felt replete

Of you bending down to tie my shoe laces
Despite grandmother's recriminations
That I was too old for such mollycoddling
You looked up and gave me a wink, your hazel green eyes twinkling
Of feeding me pungent spoonfuls of ground almonds, black pepper and honey
While I wheezed, and my asthma peaked
You held my small hands and tried to be funny
As I nestled into your tall, still athletic frame and was cherished

Of running into your study in the early mornings
Where you sat rested after your daily prayers
Waiting for me, to go for a walk with our faithful black lab, Maxie

After you were gone
I sat in your dark maroon leather chair often
Surrounded by your books
And a sweet smell of blossoms
Was that you?
Telling me that I was not alone?

What precious gifts we were to each other
You, standing in for an absent father
And I, allowing you to express unreservedly
The tenderness you did not have time for with your own progeny

So, my darling Nana
I continue to honor you and your legacy
Both in deed and memory

# NANI

It is seven years now
Since I smelt your Jean Naté perfume
And snuggled into the soft contours
Of your loving protection

Your naughty laughter ascended from a rotund belly
As you recounted riveting stories
Of the Second World War and our colorful family
Tales of mystic saints, jinns, bandits, and royalty
You were the life of the party

Blessed with a searing intellect and wondrous creativity
I witnessed your brilliant extemporaneous speeches
Mesmerize audiences and enthrall them to pieces
You were not only my beloved grandmother
But equally my mentor and teacher

You were also a gourmand, like me
And we shared many a delicious meal
At ease in your full-figured body
You never let it be an excuse to be somebody
Fearless. Respected. Opinionated. Authentic
With a will of steel

A champion of women's rights
Was a cause for which you worked tirelessly all your life
From the time you were young
A passionate advocate with both fervent pen and fiery tongue
You were a five-foot round ball of vitality
Cramming your days in service to humanity

But also quiet and reflective
As we sat on the veranda by the bougainvillea tree
Contemplating the monsoon rains
You told me how scared you were of death
And would fight it with your last breath

This fear of the inevitable
Was at odds with your deep faith in the impenetrable
And the frank admission
Of your considerable powers of intuition

Then one day, I got that dreaded call
That immortality was about to make landfall
I prayed for you to hold fast and stall
And you heard my appeal
Waiting for our last farewell

As your life ebbed little by little
I held your shriveled hand in the hospital
No longer able to speak
Communicating with our eyes
We smiled, embraced, and cried
I told you not to be afraid
As tears drifted down your wizened face

In our final hug
Your body was cold to my warm touch
But I knew I could let go peacefully
Because Nana awaited you on the other side, eagerly
And as you soar together in eternity
I know that you are both watching over me

# THE BOUGAINVILLEA TREE

I was planted in 1963
Into a square patch of brown earth
In the corner of this interior courtyard
Open to the blue sky
Since then, I have kept the rooms of this house around it company

For over 50 years now
I have been a silent witness
To the secrets, joys, pain, and loneliness
As my delicate branches coiled up to the edge of the roof
I tried to remain aloof

But my fuchsia flowers
Dappled with white and orange streaks
Gave such pleasure to my human kin
That I could not help but fall in love with my two custodians

Father, I knew for only eighteen years
He ensured that my boughs were properly trimmed
And that I got all the nourishment I needed
As I grew unimpeded
But one stifling, October morning
When I heard the lamentations
I drooped in desolation

Mother sat wakeful through the dark night
But twenty paces away from me
Sitting in the veranda on her favorite wooden rattan chair
With a broken-hearted stare
Reminiscing

Oh, how I wished I could have hugged her
As we shared stories together
Of fabulous parties and glasses tinkling
As elegant guests floated through
These now empty spaces, happily mingling

For thirty years I kept vigil
Over Mother's solitude
In gratitude
That we could still be together
For the monsoon showers that went on for days
And the long spells of dry heat that left me crazed
As the years seemed to pass by as quickly as a toddler's rage
But one bleak night Mother fell
And thereafter her room became her cell
I willed my adoration towards her still
Through the thick hospital walls
Until I felt in my roots that she was no more

Tomorrow, they are coming to hack me down
To make room for new responsibilities
I have heard their quiet whisperings

But as I shudder with fright
And try and be brave with all my might
Father and Mother appear in my dreams
With reassurances that all is not as it seems

I am so happy to see their gentle faces!
And as the first, sharp blow strikes
They encircle my withering branches
In an avalanche of boundless Love

And as I gaze below
I see five strong men
Lifting up my corpse-like form
As they struggle to take me out of what was once my home

But now I ascend upwards to a new abode
With Mother and Father by my side
I know I will never be alone

# TREADMILL GRIEVING

For many years, my relationship with food has been tumultuous
If ever there was a roller coaster built on my highs and lows
The ride would be dizzyingly ridiculous
The circular journey of dieting and exercise
Where time keeps collapsing back on itself
Like folding egg whites into a fluffy batter for a delicious cake

My step-father was a frequent companion on this voyage
As he, too, succumbed to the battle of the bulge
We often teased each other, repeatedly asking
"So, do you think I have lost any weight?"
He and I both shed and put on the kilos routinely
And the year that he died, healthy food was what he fervently ate
Even starting spinning classes, which none of us did anticipate

But who knew?
That he would be taken from us so unexpectedly
Packing all his favorite Buddha Bar CDs
To play while away on holiday
Making plans for next month. And the next
Smiling at his granddaughter
Clasping her tiny hand in his
And as he leaned against the side of the swimming pool
A hand to his chest
Then on the way to the hospital, his body convulsing next to my mother
Who knew that he would be taken away so soon

At just 54 years old, I felt his time with us had been curtailed
But when I later examined his birth and death certificates
They revealed something of great significance
He was born on a Saturday
And died on a Saturday
Time of birth – 1:45pm
Time of death – 1:45pm
What more proof did I need?
That his cycle of life was complete
But in these perplexities
The head and the heart sometimes journey
On different trajectories

Bereavement is a strange animal
It digs deeper and deeper into your soul
Finding a comfortable position in which to make its home
And in its little niche it stays forever
Because time does not heal, it just makes the pain more familiar

So, in my anguish I retreated into the arms of a faithful friend – the treadmill
In the past, it had provided a welcome distraction
From really sitting with uncomfortable emotions
But as I started walking, all the pain that was bottled up
Began pouring forth from within, like an overflowing measuring cup
Because for mourning there can be no calibrating

With each step, the wall of denial began to crumble
As I continued to stride, I felt his reassuring hand on my shoulder and was humbled
I wailed and broke apart
For the first time, I walked not with my feet but with my heart

In all my years of ambivalence to physical activity
I never thought I would use it as an artery
Both into and out of lamenting the loss of a loved one leaving
This was my treadmill grieving

# THE BUTTERFLY

It has been 8 years since we last met
But I have not forgotten you as yet
Despite the lack of news
"I pray he is keeping well," I often muse

Then last night, as the wish to see you resuscitated anew
I observed that a butterfly had appeared out of the blue
Coming to rest on the window sill
It seemed to chuckle, "You see! I am with you still!"

And today, nearly 500 kilometers away
Standing in this forest's verdant display
I see the same pulsation
Of black, white, and orange-crimson

As the butterfly continues to shadow my walk
I think of all the missed opportunities for wholehearted talks
When I longed to remove the "step" from daughter
Did you ever think of crossing out the "step" from father, too?

We had once strolled together down these green, meandering arteries
But were still burdened by the armory
Of adjusting to a new nuclear family

But today, how we could have embraced!
With hearts softened and formalities erased
Amongst the spirits of the trees and the buzz of the bees
Blessing this newfound peace

But wait!
While the gray rocks are immobile and firm beneath my feet
I know that above is another reality just as concrete
Fluttering to draw me into its affection
Of black, white, and orange-crimson

# TASTY TREAT

## IT'S A CINCH LEMON AND MINT

1/2 cup sugar

3/4 cup fresh lime juice

1/2 a big bunch of mint

2 to 2½ liters of cold water

Himalayan black salt to taste (but at least 1 teaspoon)

Pinch of black pepper powder

Blend all the above together. Adjust the seasoning according to taste. As a shortcut, squeeze large batches of fresh lime juice and freeze in ice cube trays. They will be ready at hand whenever a cooling lemon and mint drink needs to be whizzed up on a hot day.

# DESSERTS AND INFUSION

# LUMINOSITY

Turquoise sea
Lime green trees
Cinnamon sand
And just beyond, a possibility

The days are circular
Kneading together the familiar ingredients of routine
To make a perfect recipe of uniformity

Until I am jolted by purity
"Mama, does Google know everything?" asks my 5-year-old son
"I believe so."
"Except where God lives," he affirms
"And where is that?" I startle
"On a bright star, far, far away."
"And also in our hearts, don't forget," I ruminate
"Oh yes! But you would have to shrink yourself to get in there," he giggles.

Black is black. White is white
2+2= 4
And God is just a heartbeat away
How I long for such a world of simplicity!

But instead, it is filled with paradoxes
Shrinking and dilating
Growing and dying
"Yes!" And "No!"
A patchwork of perplexities

In which I am unable to feel comfortable in my body one day
And hate it the next

Get stuck in my head in the morning
But be present within myself by the evening
Taking in gratitude in one expansive inhale
And feeling lost and alone in the next exhale
I become tangled in the dualities

All I long for are some filaments of self-trust
To pull me back to that secret place within
Sitting in the shadow of the Beloved
Surrendering
With humility

I catch a glimpse of it sometimes
Just beyond the horizon
A luminosity
If I shrink myself
Will I be able to enter it, too?

# THE LIGHT OF MOSES

The cascading pronouncements
In an ecstasy of creativity
Do nothing but trap you in your own artistry

Is it really connection with the reader for which you conspire?
Or praise and admiration?
Brews headier than any magical potions

These fine poems are but adornments of
Your own pomposity
So, beware of their trickery!

Remember what the sages warn
Within us all is a Pharaoh
Full of pride and arrogance
Hypnotizing in his magnificence

He feeds on your secret desire for adulation
Growing bloated with the flattery and appreciation
This is not true ingenuity

For that, look to the wisdom articulated by a child
Only just learning to read
"One"; "When"; "Have"; "Some"
Who contemplates in the back seat
During the school run one morning

"Mama, when I grow up I want to be an astronaut.
So I can come see you, Dad, Grandma, and everyone
I love in my rocket ship."
"What do you mean?" comes your astonished reply
"When you all go back to God, of course! It's so far
away. But don't worry, I will come visit," he comforts

That is the pure light of Moses
To lead you from slavery to freedom
The simple spark of divine grace within us all
Beneath the embellished prose
To be nourished with patient humility
And become transformed
From a galloping cleverness to wordless tranquility

# GEM BONES

"Mama, did you know there are recipes for humans, like there are recipes for cooking?"
I observe the pensive look on my young son's face and wait, intrigued
"And we have gems in our bones."
"You mean like the sparkling stones?" is my query
"Yes! So, while angels are dancing lights of different colors, humans have it hidden in their clay."
At this point, I really don't know what to say

There has been a death of a loved one in the family
And it has animated my son's curiosity
What happens to the body?
And what if there is no one present to bury it?
And then what about the flesh and blood and bones?
I put a stop to the questioning, and remind him
That we are more than our outer form

"Oh yeah, the special light," he intones
"Do you know where it has its home?" I inquire
Wondering what his little mind will disclose
"It's locked in the center of your heart, of course!"
"Really?" I reply, in awe
"And the guard angels pick it up and carry it back once you die."
"Back to...?"
"Heaven, silly! If you came from heaven that is. But if not, then where you were made.
In any case, God decides," he continues to clarify

His explanation leaves me perplexed
But there is one fact I cannot contest
That we are indeed a kaleidoscope of ingredients
Anger, self-pity, anxiety, and shame
Love, hope, gratitude, and compassion
But which ones are the dominant seasonings
Are determined by our own reasonings
The choice, whether sweet or sour
Remains ours
Although in truth we need to be infused in both
To extract the richest flavors for our growth

And after our cooking time is completed
And the Light has been set free and transported
I am comforted by the notion
That we leave behind our imprint of precious gem bones

# RECYCLING

My son comes bursting through the front door
"Mama, have you finished your poems book?"
"Yes, I think so. Why sweetie?" I ask encouragingly
"I have something more I have to tell you. It's about recycling."
Intrigued by his train of thought
I ask him to proceed

"Do you know that there are things you can recycle apart from glass, paper, and plastic?"
"Hmmm... You mean also metal and cardboard?" I inquire
"Maybe. But Mama, everyone can also be recycled. Even you. Because everyone exists forever. When you
die, you are remade. You don't exist in one place, but you exist in another place," my son informs
I have heard his variations on this theme before
But nonetheless, I remain amazed

"Oh, and one more thing," he continues. "Love can also be recycled. When love breaks, you can get it
back, with the same or a different person. If you are good at handling love, it will stay. If you are bad, it
comes and goes. But if you are terrible, the love that comes goes away forever."
So, now my 6-year-old is a relationship coach?!
I am ready to throw away all my books
And listen only to his gobbledygook

There is truth to what he says
When applied also to our emotions
Many recycle sabotaging sentiments
Stuck in their stories
Colored by self-defeating perceptions
Not realizing that if they change what something means
With a more empowering interpretation
They can turn around their feelings
It is a matter of interrupting the destructive rotations
To build a new road
Towards a more fulfilling and remodeled abode

To be transformed from one shape to another
Reborn with a deeper awareness of ourselves and our relationships
Requires both effort and grace
Just as a gem cutter reveals the beauty of a precious stone
Sometimes we need to be broken open to be made whole

# DIELESS

I finish reading my son a few pages from Dr. Seuss
And after a long day
I am more than ready for a good snooze
When he chirps up
"Mama, do you know we are dieless?"
Out of the blue
His new word leaves me feeling askew

"Whatever do you mean sweetie?"
With sleepy eyes, he continues
"When we die on Earth, the guard angels come to take us up to heaven. We live there forever. All the people you love are there Mama."
"Like your great-grandparents?" I manage to croak
"Of course!" he confirms. "And when you feel sad, you can ask them to come down.
But you will only feel them in your heart, not on the outside."

The stone in my dry throat thaws
Like a rose
Composed
Of exquisite strawberry gelato
And even though I cannot fathom the probable cause
Of such a profound revelation
I am very reassured

Because you see
It is indeed to my beloved grandparents
That I turn
To resource me
When overwhelmed by life's maelstroms
They are the solid anchors
Stabilizing my unsteady trajectory

I hope that from this simple tale
You, too, can take solace
Quieting your mind
And lowering the walls around your heart
So loved ones may pay you a visit sometimes
Knowing that within that deep stillness
There is a devoted lifeline

# TODAY'S LESSON

It is the eve of another forty-something birthday
I am feeling most grateful
Despite the ups and downs of these many decades
And my happiness is homegrown

I smile at my young son's pensive reflection in the car's rear-view mirror
And so begins another enlightening exchange
As the two of us make our way back to the house

"Sweetheart, you and your sister are my beginning and my end. I love you!"
"Mama, you are my beginning, my middle, and my end! And I love you too! ... But I love God more," he intones
"Of course, and so you should," I concur
"You told me you are part angel, so do angels love God more than humans?" I continue to inquire
"No. About the same. But your big love is little for us. Because we know God properly."
"Oh, really?"
"Yes, Mama. If you loved God like we do, you would go crazy! And keep on hugging and kissing everything!"
"But isn't love a good thing?" I postulate
"Not if it makes you crazy!" he squeals
This is quite an opening
And I am curious to do a bit more snooping
"So, tell me darling, is God a boy or a girl?"
"Well actually Mama, He is a very bright light. But He can be whatever you want. Tall or short. Boy or girl. As long as you love Him."
I feel my breath catching in my throat
"And Mama," his wise little voice instructs, "If you trust Him and ask Him, then it is your right. But if you don't trust Him and ask Him, then it is not."
"What do you mean by 'right' dearest?"
"To do something Mama. Like for one person to be a cop and another, the hero."

And thus ends my lesson for today.

# TASTY TREAT

## THIS DATE TART IS A WORK OF ART

150 grams digestive biscuits, finely crushed

60 grams unsalted butter, and extra for greasing pan

400 grams date paste

1/2 teaspoon baking soda

1/4 cup boiling water (or more if needed)

Orange rind of one orange

50 grams walnuts

100 grams Lindt dark chocolate (or any other good quality dark chocolate)

200 grams condensed milk

50 grams whipping cream

1. Put a whole, unopened tin of condensed milk into a pan of water filled to about an inch above the top of the can, and boil over medium flame, covered for about 30-40 minutes. Then let it cool. Measure out 200 grams in a bowl and lightly mix with the cream. Keep aside.

2. Soak the walnuts for about half an hour. Then dry and roughly chop and keep aside

3. Preheat oven to 180 degrees Celsius.

4. Lightly butter a 12" x 7" pan and line base with parchment paper.

5. Melt the butter on a low flame and add the finely ground digestive biscuits. Mix well, pat the mixture onto the base of the pan and press it down. Put the pan in the oven and bake for 5 minutes.

6. Break the chocolate into pieces and sprinkle evenly over base. Put into oven for 2-3 minutes to soften the chocolate. Remove from oven and spread the chocolate over the base. Refrigerate until hardened.

7. Put the date paste into a bowl and add the baking soda, orange rind and hot water. Let soften for about 10 minutes, then mix together.

**Putting together:**

1. Spread the softened date mixture onto the hardened chocolate.

2. Spread chopped walnuts over date mixture.

3. Evenly pour the condensed milk mixture over the walnuts.

4. Bake for about 20 minutes or until tart begins to bubble and gets brown spots.

5. Cool, remove from pan (you can refrigerate to harden it further). Sprinkle icing sugar on top for decoration.

This rich dessert is delicious served with a dollop of vanilla ice cream. I sometimes use the dates from the trees in my garden when in season to make the paste, but it does not come out as smooth. Prepared date paste is available in many health food stores.

# INFUSION

## GINGER GREEN TEA

1 level teaspoon loose leaf green tea

1/2-inch ginger

500 ml (about 2 cups) boiling water

Organic honey to taste


Pound the ginger and add to boiling water in a teapot. Then add the green tea and brew for three minutes. Strain and add the organic honey to taste.

# AFTERWORD

I am grateful that I was able to give voice to these poems at this phase in my life. Indeed, I am humbled by the fortuitous timing of their birthing. The ages of my son (5 to 6 years) and daughter (early teens) coincide with challenging moments in my childhood that had left behind a young one who was in much need of reassurance and tenderness. However, I did not in those instances have the skills to turn towards my pain with kindness and curiosity, and instead used food to numb it.

In survival mode, I put up a protective bulwark of beliefs and behaviors that gave me a sense of being in control and safe. This was a false sense of security, creating a fragmented psychic structure, swaying precariously atop fear, expectations, judgments and compulsions for many, many years. The gentle, meandering stroll through these poetic excavations finally brought me back to the sacred space where the little one has been patiently waiting for my arrival all this long while.

Dismantling this unsteady edifice for me was linked to making peace with my dysregulated eating — the nuts and bolts I used to anesthetize emotional discomfort. Because any mental and behavior patterns based on avoidance of psychological pain are a doorway to healing it. Thus, I had to become both emotionally and physically conscious and present in my own life, taking care of myself in nurturing ways. This meant stopping dieting and listening instead to my body's wisdom and internal cues for hunger and fullness, as well as eating what felt right and gave me satisfaction.

Accepting my body exactly as it is now and letting go of judgment both for it and my feelings were also critically important. This path is not always easy, but real growth takes root in the friction between the stillness of transformation and the panic of wanting to run away and hide. I picture my emotional disquiet as a silvery ball of cotton candy that I swallow, as the undigested pain is purified and released through the heart with only a cloying sweetness remaining.

For me, this is the sweet embrace of the Beloved. As my son reminded me, "Mama, your soul is you. Your flesh and bones are what you look like. They are like your shirt and pants." My heart has known this truth since his age and earlier, but with time it was eclipsed by the constructed veils of conditioning and the illusion of separation. However, with such gentle hints, I am hopefully less likely to forget, trusting the process and leaning back without resistance into the waiting and supportive arms of the Invisible.

# ABOUT THE AUTHOR

On her own decades-long journey with emotional eating, Tameen realized that her relationship to food had not occurred by accident. A personal growth enthusiast, she was committed to finding her way through it while honoring this process. And now, she is passionate about helping others to see that their dysregulated eating has a purpose — as a powerful signpost, a message that it is time for change, to finally reach a place of peace and understanding with food.

Her law degree equipped her with the ability to think more deeply and innovatively, while her time spent in the Corporate Communications and Public Relations fields helped her to connect genuinely with people from all walks of life. Robbins-Madanes Training, where she is certified as a Strategic Intervention Coach, also provided her with a methodology for transformation and growth. But it was her own life experiences that were the spark for her search for answers.

Tameen is a devoted mother to two beautiful children. She has been a resident of ten different countries from the Indian subcontinent to Europe, the Far East, the United States, and to the Middle East. Growing up in a multi-cultural household, she was able to experience firsthand a wide range of cultures and backgrounds, affirming her belief in our common humanity and connectedness. These personal narratives have given her the unique strength to instinctually see past the outer labels we often put on ourselves instead of nurturing our shared, deep-seated, vital emotional and spiritual needs.

*Empowering transformation bridging mind and heart*

www.TameenFaridi.com

www.ingramcontent.com/pod-product-compliance
Lightning Source LLC
La Vergne TN
LVHW081327060426
835513LV00012B/1217